Evensong

BROOKS FIRESTONE

First Edition.

Published by Grundoon Publishers

Copyright © 2012 by Brooks Firestone
Cover Art by Rich Allen and Rise Delmar Ochsner

Requests to the Publisher for permission should be addressed to info@ evensong.com or visit www.evensong.com.

ISBN-10: 146 379 2867
ISBN-13: 978 146 379 2862

Printed in the United States of America

ACKNOWLEDGMENTS

My gratitude overflows for all who helped me to sing and to write Evensong:

To my voice teachers, Peter and Jody Beneke, Rose Knoles, Nichole DeChaine, John Ballerino, Ken Ryals, Ron LiPaz, Temara Brevard, Andrew Sackett, and Dan Turner.

To all the conductors and music directors, but especially Jo Anne Wasserman of the Santa Barbara Choral Society and Rose Knoles of St. Mark's choir.

To the professionals who helped me with Evensong: Milt Kahn who encouraged me to do the project, Patrick Lo Brutto who inspired the outline and organization of the book, Rich Allen and Amanda Reed who designed the book and the cover, our friend Rise Delmar Ochsner, a painter known for her loose and lush style and colorful boldness, whose painting of singers is on the cover of Evensong, Carol Lacy who edited my manuscript, and the good people of Createspace who published the book.

To those who read the early and later drafts and offered advice and encouragement: Samantha Jessup, Jo Anne Wasserman, Jim and Charlotte Lindsey, Rev. Randall Day and Canon John Andrew, Adam Firestone and Polly Walker, and above all, Kate who put up with my dreams of singing and writing.

To all my fellow singers, who put up with me in the bass section, the whole choir when I was learning, and still do now with my greater and lesser mistakes.

*Dedicated to all the choristers
and chorus members who share the pleasure,
and also the time and hard work,
of bringing music from their voices to the world.*

Contents

Evensong

BROOKS FIRESTONE

Chapter One

EVENSONG REALIZED

• • •

KATE AND I LINED UP in the basement crypt with thirty members of the Guildford Cathedral Volunteer Choir on a cold English October evening, 2010. Kate's father, Dean Walter Boulton, had married us in Guildford fifty plus years before, and we were now returning to her former home to participate in a cathedral Evening Prayer Service, or Evensong, and realize a dream that had come to us late in life.

I was out of my league, out of my country—and out of my mind with joy and apprehension to be realizing my ambition to sing with an English cathedral choir. Guildford, an hour south of London, contains one of two major cathedrals to be consecrated in Great Britain since WWII. It has a brick exterior, soaring clean lines with generous space, is easily able to hold a few thousand people, and has splendid acoustics. A large and lively congregation attends regular worship services and many community programs; an engaging dean and a musical and friendly canon precentor head up the staff of priests. The imposing building sits high on an ancient hunting enclave, Stag Hill, overlooking the busy commuter community of Guildford.

In the town below, the venerable Holy Trinity Church presides on the High Street and was where Kate and I were married in 1958, because the new cathedral was then unfinished. We celebrate our fifty-fourth anniversary in 2012, with four children, all married, and thirteen grandchildren. On our return to the cathedral in 2010, the completed building would serve for the 6:30 p.m. Evensong with Kate and me experiencing the extraordinary pleasure to be included as guest members of the choir. How we came to be there is the subject of this book.

We filed up the stairs and quietly shuffled in a two-by-two formation to a vast, dark side aisle behind the high altar. The presiding priest led us in a short prayer, and the procession silently stepped forward behind a verger, crucifer, and two acolytes with candles. The two-hundred-member congregation stood as we were ushered up the chancel steps and into choir stalls between the cavernous nave and high altar. There were four of us low basses on one side, sitting next to the second tenors and behind the second sopranos, including Kate, and the second altos. We faced our counterpart first sopranos, first altos, first tenors, and baritones in stalls across the polished stone chancel.

In the huge and hollow cathedral silence, the choirmaster took his place in front of us and the officiant rose in his pulpit with words of welcome echoing in the vast space. I glanced at my blue-robed neighbors going through their normal drill and tried to be as relaxed as they, while looking at my sheet music with apprehension. I said a silent prayer for strength and with the earnest desire to sing not for myself, but as my offering. The priest intoned, "O

Lord open thou our lips," and we were under way.

The choir sang the response, "And our mouths shall show forth thy praise!" Our voices billowed and echoed in the cathedral, and I had a moment of emotion and attention deficit as I thought, *Wow, that sounded good.*

In the forty-five-minute service (an example of an Evensong service is written in the Appendix), we sang hymns, psalms, responses, and anthem, the short sermon escaped me in the excitement of the evening. Finally, after the concluding prayers, we processed out in silence, behind the verger with his ceremonial staff, the crucifer carrying the cross, flanked by acolytes, and lastly the cathedral clergy. Again, the congregation stood in silence as we disappeared down the side aisle. The final challenge was to avoid tripping on our long choral robes while parading down the chancel steps, but that was no problem for me, as I was floating in the excitement of accomplishing a long-desired goal. We paused in our assembly area behind the great columns for a short prayer of dismissal and then proceeded down to the crypt for disrobing and goodnights. The choir, congregation, and clergy returned into the cold, fall evening and on to their warm homes. Kate and I drove back to London in the drizzly wet weather, carefully keeping to the English "wrong" side of the road. We chatted contentedly about our old Guildford past and our present retirement days.

* * *

Briefly stated about the author: I was born into the family of my grandfather, Harvey Firestone, a farm boy who founded the Firestone Tire and Rubber Company, made industrial history, and grew a fortune. My early years were marked with affluence and family name recognition, as well as the joys and burdens of that heritage. I grew up in Los Angeles in very comfortable circumstances that left me both spoiled and confused about life. A few years of the real world and economic reality were needed to sort out my direction after somewhat muddled early years. In the 1980s our family endured the sobering experience of observing this tire manufacturing bastion of American enterprise and heritage fall on difficult times and then be acquired by a Japanese company, Bridgestone.

My first career, after a two-year Army draft, was twelve years with the Firestone Tire Company, ending in the English branch in 1971, when Kate and I decided to seek independence from the family firm. We changed our lives completely, moved from England to the California Santa Ynez Valley near Santa Barbara to establish what would turn out to be a successful winery, and lived on a financially unsuccessful but family agreeable cattle ranch. Along the way I served four years as a Santa Barbara County Supervisor and four years as a California Assemblyman, in addition to running a number of unsuccessful campaigns during twenty years of political ups and downs. In recent years, we have sold the winery as well as all ranching property and have also retired from the stressful world of politics. We retained one small winery, named "Curtis," that allows our family to continue a limited connection to the wine world. Thus, in our mid-seventies we find ourselves in the slower pace of retirement with few outside responsibilities.

Kate and I have very different backgrounds. I was cosseted and comfortable in sunny California and she was a clergyman's daughter in postwar England. I was blessed with good fortune and she earned her career success with hard work under more difficult circumstances.

Kate was born in India where her father served in the Anglican Church. She lived in Calcutta, at the bishop's large house in the cathedral compound, when her father became bishop's chaplain. She grew up happily as part of the crowded Indian city during WWII. When Japanese planes attacked the docks of Calcutta, Kate and her brother and sister ran up the cathedral tower stairs to watch the bombing excitement, until they were pulled down by anxious adults who knew it was no game. She was blessed with musicality and athleticism that drew her to ballet classes, and, by the time she was eight years old, her teachers knew she had strong potential. When the family moved back to a war-torn England, in a convoy guarded by Navy warships, her training began in earnest, and her ballet school had high hopes for a young Kate in pigtails. Her hard work was ultimately rewarded by a successful career with England's Royal Ballet.

In the fall of 1955 I joined two college pals to attend a ballet performance of *Coppelia*, danced by the Royal Ballet at the old Metropolitan Opera house in New York. The spirit of the evening compelled us to bribe one of the doorkeepers to deliver a note backstage to a dancer we had chosen from names and faces in the program. Taking a long-shot chance, the message invited her and two friends to dinner. Soon a gorgeous girl named June Leslie emerged wearing a robe over her ballet tights and sporting an intriguing, heavily made-up performance face. She must have been in an adventurous mood also because, after chatting a few moments, our invitation was accepted. Three anxious college boys waited at the stage door while the girls changed from costume to street clothes; finally three beauties emerged.

In those days we usually paired off as dates, in couples. My partner was to be Catherine Boulton, called "Kate," and we curiously eyed each other. My recollection of the scene and my vision of her is as clear today as at that first moment. I fell in love there and then. Why a man and woman share an attraction beyond and above all other personal contacts and often know this at the first meeting will remain a mystery; but it happens, and it happened at that stage door and still remains in 2012. Kate also shared this first moment with a premonition that we would spend our lives together. Kismet, destiny, the great wheel of fortune, or whatever, smiled, and that is how we began.

We are fortunate that our seventy-five-year-old state of physical and mental condition today is not dotage, and we are active and ambulatory. However, we are getting on enough to sense the approach of advanced and less active life in the not too distant future. Our friends somehow appear older, and in our decade share the sense of change and premonitions of future debilitations. My body fights heart arrhythmia that might have killed me, but now survives with a pacemaker. As do many men, I live with a prostate showing signs of the dreaded cancer. I wake at night and wait for sleep, then feel in need of joint lubrication in the morning. Kate is in better shape, but time has added some aches and ailments into her daily life also. We have lost a number of activities and know that pursuits such as skiing, cattle roping, or long bike treks are mostly memories. But we maintain ourselves in reasonable shape and are able to get around, if not run around. And into this mix of late life, choral singing made its entrance.

Kate has always been musical and sang in choirs, although singing was a minor part of her life. Unlike Kate, I had no training and very little notion of singing. Happily, at a very late time in life, sixty-five, the musical muse perched on my shoulder and wafted me into a new life of song. What the muse saw in me as a singer in the great melodic domain was hard to fathom for the first few years of my new career. Fortunately, I possessed some vocal capacity, and a serious learning effort that sometimes discourages people in later life was never a burden to me. Somehow I emerged as a workaday singer; Kate went along with the idea and also began lessons to realize her potential. We drifted together into choral singing and gradually came to realize that this new avocation was becoming an important commitment and, also, a joyful dimension in our lives.

This book is about the pleasure of an active life in one's later years, how two older married characters enjoy new adventures in their mid-seventies, the joys of choral singing, and the service of Evensong that ties all these themes together. Retirement years arrive to all of us before we want or intend; Kate and I can hardly believe that this time is at hand for us. We have learned that older marrieds, like ourselves, do well to devise late-life activities that can be nurtured and shared together. We discovered that our partnership thrives in these later years partly because we have found a passion for choral singing as a communal project. This is not a "how to" book but a "how we did it" saga. There are countless pursuits that serve well for retirement occupations, and singing is only one option among many, but it has provided Kate and me great satisfaction. It will serve here as an example of shared, absorbing, late-life activity in retirement when a good rule of living is to make the most out of what might come along.

Our time of life and singing are reflected in the Anglican/Episcopal service called "Evensong." The words and musical setting were written and designed for the early evening. It is a quiet, contemplative service, suited to the time of day, and often preferred by older people given to quieter worship, and a retreat from a frenetic and sometimes hostile world. Through the ages of time, late afternoon singing has fit the end-of-day mood, whether mumbling words in a cold, prehistoric cave, lifting shaman hands to a setting sun, or softly chanting ancient prayers and hymns. Now, in life's later years, retiring and aging are inevitable, and singing Evensong has brought us both inspiration and comfort. To be able to join the chorus has become a blessing.

All the stories and observations written in this book are from Kate's and my own experiences. We have had the good fortune to sing or hear choral singing in a number of venues in America, and also in England, Canada, Italy, Spain, Germany, and Austria in many different and interesting situations. Additionally, we have attended Evensong in various countries and settings.

As I write this, our country and the world seem to be in an Evensong time of history. There is much turmoil in America and people are apprehensive. The country is broke, California is broke, towns and counties are running out of money, and implications of the inevitable cutbacks in public spending warn of social upheaval. Angry people now demonstrate and camp out to express their frustration with the unequal distribution of wealth. Greece, Ireland, Portugal, and possibly other European countries face potential bankruptcy and bailout, and the austerity measures resulting from their insolvency is the stuff of revolutions. American troops have just returned from the longest war in our history in Iraq, we have recently fought in Libya, and are continuing to fight in Afghanistan. Additionally, we are in constant fear of Muslim extremist terrorists who do what they can to hurt us. Our economy is in the dumps and will probably stay that way for a long time. Scientists tell us that our climate is changing with world-threatening consequences. In 2012 our American culture shows signs of moral uncertainty and lack of leadership that has left us with confusion and the beginnings of anarchy, reminiscent of the decline of the Roman Empire.

America seems to be no longer building history but enduring history. A case can be made that our world's condition compares to a person's late-life period of reflection and reduced energy. Something in the line of an Evensong and a little more music will only be helpful. Meditation about who we are, where we want to go, and how we move in that direction, carried out in the setting of prayer and song, can only be positive in our modern world.

Music generates its own beauty and contains the certainty of logic and organization. Musicians play and sing together in complete cooperation and adherence to rules, standards, and usages to create works of artistic integrity. Perhaps that is why singing, particularly, brings so much satisfaction in a turbulent world. Voices together cut through all the political, cultural, economic, generational, racial, and philosophical division, and provide a healing medicine for the evening news.

Kate and I believe Jesus is who He said He is and worship is a regular part of our day. Evensong to us is a traditional communication with God and a satisfying moment in the hectic pace of our personal lives. The musical setting of the service provides an aesthetic and spiritual dimension that creates a devotional fulfillment. The traditional service of Evensong serves both as an expression of worship and an historical continuity that is reassuring in our rapidly changing era.

Singing, from an amateur choir or chorus member's perspective, has somehow escaped wide discussion in literature, except technically or in critics' reviews. There are literally millions in America engaged in some type of singing, but the activity does not receive a great amount of publicity relative to other art forms. A fictional or biographical hero might be a violinist, painter, writer, or whatever, but rarely a choral singer. When I have occasion to mention our new singing career to family and friends, they are supportive and interested, but more curious than knowledgeable about choral singing and surprised to hear our adventures. For relatively new singers, Kate and I have enjoyed a wide range of performing and listening in our short careers, which bear repeating and might even inspire others and stimulate their latent talent.

Each of us follows our own path in life, and this saga contains a good part of our personal road. This is a story of how we came to sing and what and where we have sung in our late-life careers. From our earliest moments, all of us watch and learn from observing our fellow humans. We also read about and ponder the adventures, thoughts, and experiences of others, both contemporary and historical, in order to instruct our own lives. If there is something in Kate's and my experience that can amuse or provide grist for thought to anyone, I will have served my purpose in this book.

Chapter Two

Moving On

• • •

"To everything there is a season, and a time to every purpose under the heaven...A time to weep, and a time to laugh; a time to mourn, and a time to dance" (Eccl. 3:1,4).

"For every season, turn, turn, turn, there is a reason..."

Ecclesiastes got it right and the Byrds rock band got it right. Each of us in our own way need to get it right, even as time moves on.

Kate and I were attending my former brother-in-law's seventieth birthday party given by his three adult children in his London apartment. It was a lively affair with family and friends, including three or four women he occasionally swans around with when the circumstances call for a couple, because he had been a bachelor for a few years. I was speaking with one of them, an attractive blonde, and we both were trying to be witty and slightly flirtatious with each other, as one does at a party with a glass of wine in hand. After the usual questions about why are you in London and aren't there great views from this apartment, etc., she asked me if my wife was at the party. I answered yes, and pointed out Kate. She asked me how long we had been married. I said a long while. Did we have children?

"Yes," I answered, "four."

"How old?"

I prevaricated.

No," she insisted, "how old are your children?"

"Well," I finally replied, "my oldest daughter has just had her fiftieth." The conversation paused.

"Good heavens," she exclaimed, "you're old enough to be my father." Ouch! An all-too-graphic sign of my moving on.

There are obvious road signs in the aging process. The big seventy, seventy-five, eighty, and beyond birthdays mark time. The moments of retirement from business or profession mark career passage. A number of physical hiccups from aches and pains and a creaking early-morning body gradually morph into more serious problems that bring a frown to the doctor's face, followed by earnest discussions about diet and exercise. Confusion, lost names, and other mental lapses mark the mental debilitations of aging. A myriad of changed lifestyles reflect the settling down of energy and pace. Yet, despite all these signs, most of us ignore the changes in life indicated by these markers with blessed innocence or an overly optimistic, positive attitude. We carry on as we were, holding our grasp on business as usual, entering our advanced years with our own ways of avoiding reality; but the fact is that time moves on.

Some younger people live with the notion that this stage of life will never arrive. Some older types remain in a state of denial. But there is a time when competitive athletics are a distant memory. There is a time when sex becomes largely theoretical. There is a time when conversations with friends center on physical infirmities, and sometimes reference terminal debilitations. There is a time when quieter moments become more pleasant than exciting ones, and when watching is as satisfactory as participating. There is a time when one knows the answers, but convincing others is not so important. Inevitably, distinguished good looks fade and the mirror is not much fun.

About that time we learn that the muscles do not keep up with the games our grandchildren play, and it is useless trying to follow them on a bicycle. We have all heard the expression, "Old age is not for the faint of heart," but a time will come when all of us will learn too well what that expression means. And these are the times that cry out desperately for a passionate activity to fill the voids and heal the debilitations.

Here is what we hope to avoid in this stage of our lives. Samuel Beckett wrote a brief, scathing, poignant, and sometimes all-too-true monologue play entitled *Krap's Last Tape*. The short drama involves the sordid life of a sad, aging man in the process of tape-recording his annual message, a form of yearly spoken diary. Krap is alone, bitter, hopeless, without direction, friends, or activity, and waiting to die. The play depicts a vacuous ruin of a life, profound gloom, an impoverished soul, embittered and empty. The only reason to see the play is—as the title of a Hemingway short story relates, and as we must hope for ourselves—"A Way You'll Never Be."

Appropriate to the theme of this book, Krap remembers his boyhood and mournfully bleats into the microphone, "Went to Vespers once, like when I was in short trousers," (pause, sings) "Now the day is over, night is drawing nigh-igh, shadows" (coughing almost inaudible) "of the evening steal across the sky" (gasping). "Went to sleep and fell off the pew." We can feel for the young boy, Krap, and the old man, Krap, who never sang nor listened to music; hopefully it will never be us. We will age with grace, style, action, and joy. But how?

Ernest Hemingway gave us world-class literature and insights written with unbeatable style. But, unfortunately, he gave up on the potential of retirement years. A.E. Hotchner, a close personal companion and confidant of Hemingway's, quoted a conversation with his friend toward the end of the great writer's life in his book, *Papa Hemingway*. The conversation involved the injury of a matador who would now be forced to retire, and Hemingway is quoted as saying: "The worst death for anyone is to lose the center of his being, the thing he really is. Retirement is the filthiest word in the language. Whether by choice or by fate, to retire from what you do—and what you do makes you what you are—is to back up into the grave."

The point of this book is to dare to disagree with the great man. We will inevitably retire from our jobs or professions, and we will lose much of our physical and some of our mental prowess in those retirement years. This in no way precludes the invention of a new life. And the possibility exists that the new life will be equally, or possibly more, fulfilling and vital than the earlier us.

In the modern world we are healthier longer and, accordingly, need to provide for those future years of ability and potential to maintain an active life despite what, in former generations, might be considered old age. In our youth we are compelled to seek improvements and accomplishments in our lives. We pursue education, athletic prowess, learning experiences, career, family, friends, wealth, political involvement, philosophical truths, and all the other desirable ends one strives for in the early days. Later in life, and that is much later, goals are limited but should be equally important in our lives. Then we will still need new learning quests, new physical pursuits, and new goals, certainly less ambitious than in the early years, but no less essential.

The early years should prepare for retirement years, and sooner rather than later we should search for what might become a passionate involvement, and also develop the skills for the later fulfillment of that avocation. Whether it is to be stamp collecting, gardening, dog showing, or a host of other possible pursuits, one should ponder what that involvement might be. Planting even a few seeds in early years in order to harvest a late-life expertise might be the best investment an individual can make. Marathon running and sky diving might not be manageable in one's seventies, except for a daft and gifted few, but we all have individual tastes and talents that might well serve our reduced capacities. For example, Kate and I regret that we did not study music or singing earlier, and were extraordinarily lucky that this late-life passion seemed to find us. Perhaps we are living proof that it is better to be lucky than intelligent, but we should have been better prepared for our retirement. Most young people plan for financial stability for the retirement years, but there is also a real need for activity planning.

Some years ago three couples, including four medical doctors from Sioux City, Iowa, purchased a stay in our vineyard at a local wine event charity auction. The idea was to learn about harvesting grapes and making wine over a long weekend, as our guests, but they spent a minimum of time winemaking. They were delightful people and shared a mutual passion to which they preferred to dedicate their vacation time: cooking. They were happiest spending hours in our kitchen preparing soups, main dishes, and desserts with timeless absorption. With a surgeon's precision, they sliced, diced, pulverized, blended, sampled, basted, and gloriously kitchen-messed an entire morning away, while sharing and comparing culinary techniques and food gossip. Their meticulous attention to ingredients and detail, seeking preparation perfection beyond any commercial chef's dreams, was a joy to behold. The resulting meal was truly spectacular. We marveled and toasted their skills and passion, knowing that these people enjoyed the timeless gift of a shared enterprise that would see them happily through life.

There are compensations in later life for the loss of youthful health and energy. Hopefully, there will be adequate retirement resources that will allow career anxieties to be forgotten; what bliss to be out of the rat race! At last there is the time for family, now more precious in the leisure years, and particularly with grandchildren. Friends enrich our lives now that we have time and to enjoy one another's company. There is less concern about wealth or status because the treasure chest is as full at it will ever be, and recognitions and accolades just do not matter. The end game hovers, but in those golden years, now more lengthy and vital than any previous generation, the most precious experiences are also waiting.

Rudyard Kipling wrote an oft-repeated poem, "If," which included the famous admonition, "If you can fill the unforgiving minute with sixty seconds worth of distance run..." Our challenge is to make these minutes count, with the added bonus that, by filling them with vital activities, we also add more than a few minutes to our time on earth.

Too often retired people, even accomplished professionals, promise themselves travels, vacations, and luxuries once they have lifted their noses from the grindstones of their careers. The moment arrives and one or two years of sumptuous rewards and indulgences are enjoyed, but the supposed good life wanes, and the driven, skilled individuals face an unrelenting quiet and trouble-free—but suspiciously dull—future. Often these capable and successful people, having enjoyed a rewarding intermission, simply go back to their original profession for lack of challenge or activity to match their energy. High living is good for awhile, but there must be more.

One friend, after a highly successful advertising career, woke up from a quiet and comfortable retirement to throw his talents into heading up a local hospital fund-raising campaign. Another friend, a retired airline pilot, has devoted his every free retirement minute into building a small airplane. His wife hopes he will never finish and attempt to fly the project. A local retired CEO of a defense contracting company fills his life with a woodworking shop, turning out beautiful gifts for family and friends—and a healthy scar from his band saw. These gently aging individuals are happy and fulfilled with their new careers.

Retirees often develop a passion for accumulating a collection of something. The wine trade has long marveled at wealthy individuals who accumulate vast cellars that will surely outlive the collector. Similar to rare stamp collections, the wine labels and vintages take on a fervent importance to the avid assembler, and auctions thrive from the need to fill the bins with historic wines. Often these cellars grow too large and valuable for the simple enjoyment of consumption, and languish, pristine and unconsumed, in temperature controlled splendor. It would seem that as a retirement activity, the collector's passion serves only as a sideshow and not the main event.

An example of what can be pursued in a late-life second career stands in North Phoenix, Arizona, as a musical treasure that grew from one man's personal inspiration. The Musical Instrument Museum, or MIM, that opened in 2010, is destined to become one of the important museum destinations in America. The founder, Robert Ulrich, has been a lifelong collector of African art and an aficionado of museums. During a trip to Belgium he decided to found a musical instrument museum. Since, retiring as chief executive and chair of the Target Corporation, he has pursued this dream. He has put his considerable management skills and personal wealth to good use, resulting in this fascinating collection and unique display of international, historical, and contemporary instruments that rose from the desert floor. Now, in retirement years, he devotes his considerable wealth and talents to insuring that MIM is a world-class experience. He can sometimes be found following visitors through the exhibits and recording their reactions on a clipboard, meeting with senior team members of the museum, or pitching potential benefactors.

Musicians, or anyone, interested in an absorbing day experience of hearing and seeing international musical cultures, should make a pilgrimage to the MIM. Unlike many museums, one can see engaging smiles on the visitors' faces and rapt attention to the exhibits. My personal reaction was similar to my visit to the new Cathedral in Barcelona: there are great and meaningful works still to be celebrated and anticipated in the world. At an age when many begin to think of a quieter life, Bob Ulrich is accomplishing a passionate quest, and our country is a better place for his energies.

The need to fill the retirement years with activity is more pressing than ever because we are living longer and healthier. Scientists, planners, and government officials have been surprised by the startling changes in life expectancy. Just a hundred years ago, life was shorter by around twenty-five years. When Social Security was invented in the 1930s, it was based on the sound fiscal calculations of only a few people living longer than seventy-five years. Now, there is discussion of increasing the age of receiving Social Security benefits to the age of seventy. Of course we should work longer and receive benefits at a later age, firstly because we are very capable of being good workers beyond the age of sixty-five, and also because the pension system of America is heading for bankruptcy in the near future. In the next generation, life after one hundred years will more and more be the norm, and these future oldsters can absolutely expect to be brighter and more able in their seventies and eighties.

Our generation grew up thinking that the seventies were old age; but now those of us who have reached that age know that things changed, and, unlike our parents and grandparents, this stage of life is comfortable and creative. Good news can and does abound in these years.

A new scientific trend in economic studies is to quantify happiness, apart from wealth, in individuals, countries, races, cultures, and every conceivable sector of the world's population. Public policy thinkers are urging researchers to measure well-being, both in terms of financial and material possessions, and separately, in terms of people's sense of a positive and satisfied attitude about their lives. Fascinating new insights emerge, indicating that, although wealth plays a part in well-being, there are factors beyond and apart from material abundance that formulate the satisfactions of a good life. Happiness is hard to quantify and analyze, but it is real and very much a new and important area of scientific investigation. These inquiries validate our instinctual perceptions about happiness that have lived in cultural wisdom for generations. Our incessant need for facts, figures, and intellectual inquiry drive the investigations into interesting conclusions. Science is validating that you cannot buy love and you cannot buy happiness.

Economists, looking closely at what happiness—or rather the pursuit of happiness—truly means are discovering new knowledge about cultures and aging. The acquisition of material goods and conspicuous consumption as a demonstration of the good life are losing status in judging one's well-being. In Greek terms, the demonstrative *hedonic* well-being is losing out to the state of personal *eudaimonia*, or outer directed and fulfilled well-being. Simply put, the satisfactions of building a birdhouse might be healthier and more important to happiness than having a Ferrari in the garage. People have always said those things, but scientists are quantifying the data and confirming the perceptions.

Also, a new theory of the "U-Shaped Life Happiness Curve" brings good news to us in our senior years. It seems as though we are well content in childhood, but this happiness declines in adolescence, and continues to slide through most of our working lives. The cares of careers, new families, and all the stress of the thirties and forties, which folks discover in their lives, bring them to the nadir of the happiness curve. Gradually, with maturity, people become happier until breaking through in retirement, when those who have reached seventy and eighty years are measured to be happiest of all. Now it should be understood that this is a new field of science, and no theory can account for so many individual variations of the world's people. However, early indications and data are very positive for us older types.

Krap did not know how to live or how to fill the full sixty seconds of every minute with life. Let us all seek a happy and fulfilled minute.

Chapter Three

$\mathcal{B}$ROOKS $\mathcal{S}$INGS

● ● ●

IN ALL MY SEVENTY-FIVE YEARS I had never felt as nervous and stressed as I was in July 2006 when Kate and I were auditioned for membership in the Santa Barbara Choral Society. I felt helpless, inadequate, frightened, and totally apprehensive. Kate had been through auditions all her professional dancing life, so it was business as usual for her.

The routine for auditions, I had been informed, was that we would schedule our appointment time, check in at the Montecito Presbyterian Church Hall, and, on schedule, present ourselves to an evaluating committee. This year, the auditioning would be done by a panel headed by the music director, Jo Anne Wasserman, an assistant conductor, tenor John Revheim, baritone Steve Dombek, alto Linda Rouhas, and soprano section leader Tamara Brevard. The sympathetic pianist, Carol Roberts, was ready to be helpful at the grand piano but, otherwise, the group awaiting us singers seemed formidable. I had been taking voice lessons from Tamara for nearly a year, and she snuck me a smile as I entered the large church hall, the only friendly face in the otherwise hanging jury. Since then, I have become good friends with them all, but at the time I felt only the innocent terror of a sacrificial lamb in the abattoir. It is interesting that, since that audition year, there has never again been a committee assessing the voices, because the membership felt the committee system was too intimidating.

The foundation of a singing group, and its quality of sound, is the talent of the voices, determined in the first instance by the audition process. A pick-up songfest in a bar will be whoever happens along, no musical test, drinks all around. A Rotary Club with their songbook and a modicum of leadership might be the next step, but still no audition. Somewhere beyond this are singing organizations open to all, and school choirs that include any student, that are organized for teaching basic music. An un-auditioned and welcome-to-all church choir will probably be next on the scale, although these vary greatly according to the tradition and dedication of the church and members. For instance, our local St. Mark's choir is open to anyone who wishes to join; nevertheless our standard is relatively high for a church choir, and one who cannot learn an anthem quickly and maintain pitch will probably not want to continue. At the top is a comprehensively and critically auditioned chorus that also reviews the singing experience of the applicant, and admits only very qualified singers.

Choral groups become known by their auditions. An encouragingly friendly review of potential singers, such as the Lompoc Master Choral, maintains a reasonable quality of sound; but a strict audition, such as the Santa Barbara Choral Society, presents a tougher challenge. Auditioning in a famous choral group, such as the Atlanta Symphony Chorus or the Los Angeles Master Chorale, might include solo songs, interviews, and a record of past performances. When dealing with a voluntary organization, and the individual egos and personalities of the potential members, the process can go hard on both the singer and the evaluator who must inevitably make the tough decision and, if need be, disappoint the applicant. There are around a hundred singers in the Santa Barbara Choral Society who have successfully been through the audition process, and many more who have not succeeded in the audition. Accordingly, the Society has held a high standard and solid reputation.

It is generally understood that men have an easier time in auditions simply because there are more women who sing. The soprano and alto sections are usually filled, while a chorus will almost always be looking for tenors and basses. This notion gave some comfort to the men who faced the Choral Society audition trauma. People can sing into a well-advanced age, but everyone has their time of failing voice, and some who have sung with the chorus for many years had some reason for concern, since all members are re-auditioned every other year.

During my audition day, in an effort to mitigate the strains of the moment, the Choral Society scheduled two singers to be evaluated together in the large church hall. My auditioning partner was to be a friendly Doctor Gil Asher, a regular with the Choral Society bass section. We met and I said to myself, *If he can do it I can do it*, but I did not entirely believe this.

The tests are designed to find out who can hold the pitch of a note correctly, who can read music, and who can sing the designated written notes in the company of other singers using different written parts. The entry level of the audition begins with a basic scale; then singing to match notes played by the piano in a random pattern. The reviewers listen, in this first test, to see if a singer can replicate a note and also produce a tone that will blend with the other singers. If the notes are out of tune or the tone is harsh or aggressive, the applicant will probably be confined to listening as a member of the audience. The two of us went up and down the scale individually and then matched random patterns played on the piano.

Additionally, the audition assesses a singer's confidence in singing publicly, because there must be a self-assurance and ability to perform in front of an audience. If a snow skier peers down a steep downhill run with doubt, the day is liable to end in the hospital. Safe skiers lean down the mountain with a confident exhilaration. Likewise, in steeplechase racing, horse and rider approach a hurdle at an impossibly high speed and start the jump from a mind-blowing distance to fly the fence. A nanosecond of doubt can be transmitted to the horse, resulting in a broken-bone tumble, or ignominious stop with the rider flying through the air. Confidence is everything in so many endeavors, and very much a factor in singing. Choral applicants must confront the audition with the assurance that the note will come loudly, clearly, and enjoyably.

My moment came, I breathed deep and lit the airwaves with an accurate and well-shaped middle C. I would survive.

The next test was our ability to read music. We were given a booklet and asked to turn to page eight and sing the indicated piece along with the piano. Here our nervous duet hit rocks and shoals. Gil turned to the wrong page, and my eyes fixed on the lower music line, where I thought the bass part would be, rather than the upper line that was the beginning. I did not realize that all lines on the page were bass and it was intended that I should begin at the top. The piano merrily started off on the little piece while Gil sang the wrong song and I sang the wrong line. The music director, Jo Anne, waved us off, "There seems to be some confusion here!" and there were nervous laughs all around. We finally sorted ourselves out and launched correctly into the innocent song, reading the notes for the first time as best we could.

Next came the most dreaded test: rhythm. We were given a tricky tune on a music sheet and asked, individually, to count in rhythm the eighth, quarter, and half notes, remaining silent in the rests. We both stuttered and floundered. After more nervous glances we moved onto the final test, singing in parts.

A friend, Bob Lally, who had sung in the bass section for years, had slipped me the word that the song to be used was a venerable, beautiful, and uncomplicated piece composed by a musician in Henry the Eighth's court, Thomas Tallis, entitled "O Nata Lux." At the time, I was serving as a Santa Barbara County Supervisor, and my office was downtown in the county building. On the morning of my audition, my administrative aide, infinitely more computer-savvy than I, found a reproduction of the piece on the county computer. We closed the office doors, which he faithfully guarded, while I vocalized the short song, time after time, to the strains squawked out by the computer. I finally gained a degree of confidence in the music, and could sing the Latin words from memory by the time of my afternoon appointment.

O *Nata Lux de lumine*	O light born of light
Jesu redemptor saeculi	Jesus, redeemer of the world
Dignare Clemens supplicum	Mercifully deem us worthy
Laudes preces que sumere	To offer prayers and praise
Qui carne quondam contegi	You who once deigned to become flesh
Dignatus est pro perditis	For the sake of your lost ones

Nos membra confer effici	Grant that we become members
Tui beati corporis	Of your holy Body.

I had come to enjoy the beautiful song, but then Kate, who was also scheduled for audition, showed up with an entirely different piece of music. A friend of hers had discovered that the "O Nata Lux" to be sung was by a modern composer, Morton Lauridsen, and she had secured a copy. The music sheet was complicated and impossible to learn in the car while driving to the appointment: a rendezvous that I was now sure would end my musical career. Frantic despair caused me to break out in panicked sweats. I wanted very much to sing with the Choral Society and had worked two years for the audition—which now seemed like the gallows.

Our test had reached the point of singing the appointed piece with the committee members joining with the soprano, alto, tenor, and baritone parts, to see if we could hold our bass line while they sang different notes to harmonize. So far, Gil and I seemed to be meeting with smiles from the committee, but now the dreaded moment of performance had arrived. We were handed the sheets of music and, to my delight and amazement, discovered it was not Kate's dire prediction but my friendly Lux by Tallis! I sang with confidence and joy. The reviewers thanked us and that was the end of the audition, without a commitment one way or another.

We had more expectation that Kate would be able to handle the audition, but she insisted that we have a deal. She told me firmly that if I passed and she did not, I was welcome to sing and she would be in the audience, but if she passed and I did not, she would not join the chorus by herself. We fretted for a few days after the audition, but finally letters came inviting both of us to join the Society, and our new career was launched. Kate would sing in the alto section, although she was capable of producing the high notes of the second sopranos, and I was to be a bass. The higher notes of the baritone section probably fit me better, but the bass line is usually more straightforward and readable and thus suited my talents better.

We experienced a very different audition years later, in 2011, when the Choral Society had their annual review. We were now experienced singers and convinced that we had appreciatively improved with many lessons, rehearsals, and concerts, and approached our audition with confidence. We heard that many were very nervous about singing in front of our director, Jo Anne, and some had even cancelled their appointments and irrationally put off the moment rather than face the ordeal. When the audition arrived, we were taken in three at a time and sang at Jo Anne's instructions, with her assistant, John Revheim, playing the piano. Again, scales, matching notes, sight-reading, rhythm counting, and singing together were the tests. Both Kate and I went in with our section members, full of confidence, sang boldly, and were totally shattered to hear the tone of our voices.

We were bitterly disappointed with ourselves, and crept out of the music room. Even though we had been told that we had passed and were accepted, we could not escape feeling that we were worse singers than ever. Later, we discovered that two of our regular members were gently asked not to continue and five new members were accepted out of a dozen or so applicants. Jo Anne, kindly, told me privately that I was making good progress, but I suppose I had expected to sound like a professional and was forced to be satisfied with an amateur and nervous voice. In any case, we looked forward to another year of music.

* * *

In our first year, after being accepted in the Society, our initial rehearsal was apprehensive for me, but filled with happy reunions with the hundred or so regulars in a large room at the Music Academy. Kate was a show-business trouper accustomed to new situations, but I felt intimidated—a new boy who knew himself to be swimming well out of his depth. We began rehearsing for a *Messiah* performance and I meekly did my best, only murmuring next to my friend and mentor Bob Lally. He finally turned and said, "You're hiding, aren't you?" I guess I was.

As time and weekly rehearsals went on, I grew some confidence and, by our first concert, sang out with the rest, but not without inner misgivings. I knew I was making progress when he said, "You're beginning to fly, aren't you?" Friend Bob, I knew, suffered in hearing some atonal and arrhythmic moments from his new neighbor, but gradually I seemed to move into a modest but acceptable singing ability, and did so with a great sense of accomplishment. Sometimes Bob would give me some gentle hints or simply motion with his hand, usually in an upward direction, to point out the proper pitch, and I greatly appreciated the help. On rare occasions, he would lean into my ear and lead by example. Singing next to a competent and experienced person is very beneficial, especially to an insecure singer. I might then be called the soul of insecure.

Oddly enough, I had previously experienced a unique introduction into the world of song that should have given me confidence. For years I had been a member of a venerable wine and food society called the *Chaine des Rotisseurs*, named after the chain on the roasting spit, which numbered around 7,500 members in 140 chapters throughout the United States and many more thousands around the world. I was asked to head a committee that would make the wine activities of the organization more interesting, and our group became creative. We devised many new dimensions for this wine part of the *Chaine* society, called *L'Ordre Mondial des Gourmets Degustateurs*, or worldwide order of discriminating tasters, including an elaborate induction ceremony with the officers wearing robes, and a loyal song for everyone to sing.

The song was based on the ancient Boar's Head Carol and went something like this:

The leader would sing: "*Gustato Optimorum*, we, the Chaine assembled gallantly, I pray you my masters be merry, *Quod Estes in Convivio.*" (*Gustato Optimorum*, those who taste the best, and *Quod Estes in Convivio* roughly means everybody here be happy.)

The assembled diners would then sing, "Vintners, cooks and company: in joy at table in harmony!"

This little song may sound strange, and becomes even more exotic when we proceeded with the verse format, which allowed any individual to make up a couplet and stand up and sing. For example a dinner guest might sing out: "The Bordeaux wine with taste supreme: I think it samples like a dream," or, "We thank our host for providing this: a splendid dinner and wines of bliss."

After each made-up solo, the company would then sing, "Vintners, cooks, and company: in joy at table in harmony."

The fun and pleasure of the song may have lost something in the explanation, but, in fact, it often gave a great boost to the party and everyone had a grand time singing together at an elegant and lavish meal with more than adequate wines. When I became the president of the organization, I always found myself singing at least one solo and sometimes more. It was a gratifying experience to stand up at a Chaine Society dinner and sing, and hopefully not be too embarrassing. Over a few years I led this singing many times around the country, albeit with a few glasses of dinner wine, both for audience and performers, as a warm-up. This experience might have indicated that I could sing if I wanted to do so, and if there was enough wine available.

Additionally, as a teenager in high school, I had played the drums in a jazz band. This experience had nothing to do with formal music or reading the notes on a page, or knowing any details of what we were doing, other than improvising. But it did indicate that I had an instinct for rhythm that gave me a foundation for my future training.

My path from wine society to choral singing was marked by a gradual realization that, like many people who have never explored their latent talent, I could sing. Of course this discovery came with a good amount of study, practice, lessons, and a very slow growth of confidence. Singing ability might be compared to tasting ability. From my experience of over thirty-five years growing grapes, running a winery, and attending numerous wine tastings with professionals and amateurs, I had learned that there are many degrees of talent and discernment in tasting wine. Sometimes a total novice would wander into our winery tasting room and display an uncanny ability to recognize flavors, and match and evaluate different wines. This individual was blessed with a natural talent that could be developed or not, but was a part of that person's unique natural capacity. Similarly, many are blessed with degrees of rhythm and pitch that can be developed into musical ability or lie dormant. There are few people who do not have some capacity to sing or play music, or any number of other potential talents; and blessed are those who realize their potential. When I sense a wine taster's exceptional ability, I want to lead that fortunate person into the world of wine discernment and full enjoyment of the flavors. Likewise, I hope that everyone who can sing will open their lungs and voice to enjoy the world of making a joyful noise. Good fortune, and a smattering of an instinct that singing was possible, opened a new future and allowed me to enjoy a latent gift.

My first genuine musical step came to me late in life, when I was sixty-five years old, and by a fortuitous combination of circumstances. For years I would sit alone in the congregation while Kate sang happily in the choir. Sometimes I had a vague notion that it would be fun to join her. When good fortune comes our way in this life, happy are those who seize the moment. Good fortune entered my life in the form of a professional singer and teacher, Peter Beneke, who, with his wife Jody, also a former opera singer, joined our St. Mark's church choir. With some inclination that it might be fun to sing, in a very limited way, I hired on for lessons with Peter. My ambition was only to learn the anthem or the music to be sung that Sunday by the choir, before our rehearsal, so that I would not entirely embarrass myself with the full choir. With that preparation, I tenuously moved from the congregation to join Kate in the choir, and soon found that donning the robes and sitting with the real singers was enjoyable and well worth continuing. Ten years later I still wake on Sunday mornings, excited with the anticipation of joining in with the local St. Mark's choir.

Our church routine is to meet an hour and a half before the service. We warm up by singing a verse or two of each scheduled congregational hymn and then launch into learning that Sunday's anthem. Our hymns in the congregation's books are the standards, and two or three are sung every Sunday by both choir and congregation. The anthems are more difficult pieces, chosen from a vast compilation of religious music, written in two- or four-part harmony, and sung only by the choir.

Our rector, Randall Day, appreciates and makes good use of the choir. We are blessed with a brilliant leader in Rose Knoles who retired to choral directing after many years cultivating the musical talents of high school students. She has the ability to translate sheets of unfamiliar music into an acceptable service anthem in a very short time and with a mixed bag of singers. Sometimes I wondered whether she would give up on an ambitious piece she had chosen and fall back on a familiar standby, but she never failed to pull off the intended piece. Our choir varies from twelve on a quiet Sunday to twenty-four when there is an important service. We are never sure of the makeup of the choir, though the basses and altos are fairly predictable, but who will be in the tenor or soprano sections varies from week to week. We are a congenial group and, I believe, appreciated by the congregation.

My singing career progressed for a couple of years in the choir with a lesson every week, and I found myself gaining confidence and enjoyment. At first I depended heavily on my very able seatmate, Pete Knoles, to show me the way, but gradually I began to sing on my own.

One day, Jody Benecke, my voice teacher's wife, who headed the music department of our local community college, said to me, "You know, Brooks, if you wanted to sing more, you could probably do it. Why don't you join the Lompoc Master Chorale? We're singing a Christmas program and you might enjoy the experience." Jody conducted this chorus and thought I might fit in as a bass. Peter agreed and said he too was wondering if I would go to a different level. Kate took it all in stride and we agreed to undertake the challenge together. Neither of us knew the extent to which we were about to engage in a new world when we drove together to the town of Lompoc, about forty minutes away, to attend weekly rehearsals.

The music program was familiar and seasonal except for an amazing piece by J.S. Bach, "Wachet Auf, ruft uns die Stimme" (Sleepers Awake), that was a formidable challenge. With some trepidation, I sang the concert with the Chorale at the interesting venue of one of the original California Missions, La Purisima, just outside Lompoc. The experience of plowing through the Bach, even with indifferent success, brought me to a new level of pleasure in singing and into the world of great choral music.

We enjoyed two seasons with the Lompoc Master Chorale, but

then Jody moved to take a post as music director in a Sonoma college, and we moved on to the challenge of singing with the Santa Barbara Choral Society. I had heard them in a concert a number of times and knew their splendid abilities very well. Also, my good friend and singing neighbor in the St. Mark's choir, Pete Knoles, sang with them and had often told me about the pleasures of being a baritone in the group. He, of course, knew my tenuous musical background, and assumed that I could enjoy listening to the Choral Society concerts, but might never aspire to be part of that accomplished organization.

However, during those four years I had moved into a serious study mode. Our choir director, Rose Knoles, with her infinite talent, patience, and grace, took me on for weekly music theory lessons, gently leading me into the mysteries of reading the music sheet. Peter Beneke continued with my voice lessons, and I began coaching with a soprano from the Choral Society, Tamara Brevard. I also had a few lessons from two accomplished bass/baritones, Ken Ryals and Ron LiPaz. I told those two that all I wanted to do is sing as they did. Gradually the symbols and notes of a musical score sheet became legible, and the quality and consistency of tones being coaxed from my body gained a semblance of respectability.

When the time came that I actually could, albeit slowly and hesitatingly, accompany myself on the piano to learn a bass line of music, I entered a new level. Improving one's singing voice is an infinitely complicated and subtle combination of physical factors involving breathing and shaping the note through the vocal chords. Such terms as "singing through the top of your head," and "using your body as a tubular instrument," became vaguely familiar. Each teacher describes the mysteries of singing in a different manner—something like the subtleties of working with a golf instructor.

Finally came the Society audition and acceptance, and to my amazement I was a member of the chorus I had admired so enthusiastically from the audience. I know I will always struggle and take more time than most to learn a new piece of music. I also know that my contributions to a bass section will be that of a dedicated amateur with only a mid range of talent. But that is more than enough to fulfill my ambitions, and this labor of love has opened a world of pleasure and excitement of singing great music in an amazing array of venues, circumstances, and company.

Our first Choral Society concert was the *Messiah* by George Frederick Handel in the First Presbyterian Church in Santa Barbara. I worked for weeks every day on that piece of music, studying on my own, with a *Messiah* learning CD where the bass part is exaggerated, and with lessons three times a week with two voice teachers. Our weekly rehearsals, and then dress rehearsal with orchestra, became a joy and the sound produced by the Society began to seem quite splendid. The first rehearsal with chorus and orchestra was a mind-expanding experience and a revelation that I had entered a new level of expression and participation.

Performance day routine began with assembly in a rehearsal room in the basement of the church an hour before the concert. Men wore tuxedos and the women black concert dresses, with our music carried in standard black binders. We settled in with Assistant Director John Revheim leading us first through warm-up scales and then through some of the *Messiah* section openings and more difficult parts. We trooped upstairs to form rows outside the church, in position, to mount the risers quickly and easily. I could not help noticing that there was an almost sell-out crowd packing the church. People had paid money to hear us sing!

When we finally took our places on the risers for the concert, we found ourselves with different neighbors from our rehearsal locations. Fortunately, my security, Bob Lally, was still standing on one side, but a talented, and accomplished soprano, Diane Das, stood on my other side. She, of course, would sing the soprano line, and additionally and threateningly, she did not even open her music score. Before the final rehearsal I whispered to her, "If you don't open your music, I'll never know what page I'm supposed to be on!" She laughed and put up with me and my voice. As we took our places on the risers I had the feeling that everyone was looking directly at my shaking hands and knees.

All too soon the orchestra began, and then we were singing my first Santa Barbara Choral Society concert. I remember my initial notes were somewhat hesitant, but, as the piece wound its magnificent musical spell, I gained in confidence and sang out. Singers, and particularly new singers, live in dread of making a small mistake, rattling one's neighbors, or a big mistake that might reach as far as the audience. The least blunder is singing under or over pitch, and the most devastating is coming in decisively when only silence is called for and otherwise maintained by a hundred voices. This is called the famous "unpaid solo!"

In the first Saturday night *Messiah* we began smoothly and without a moment of hesitation or musical hiccup. As the music proceeded a change came over my very being. Gradually, I forgot about me and my nervousness, and became part of the chorus, blending with fellow basses and merging my voice and persona with my neighbors. There is a joyous moment in choral singing when one becomes conscious of being a part of the musical whole, and for the first time I experienced this combined force of the group and the surrender of one's voice to the common voice. I felt a thickening in my throat when I saw Kate in the alto section, looking beautiful and also deeply into the moment and performance.

The "Hallelujah Chorus" is the most famous part of the *Messiah*, but the most formidable and difficult section is the "Amen Chorus" that concludes the work. Something special caught on with the chorus for that portion, as we sailed and soared to a full voice climax. The audience stood and cheered, and one man actually huzzahed with his hat on his cane! Afterward, I felt drained and totally content. The chorus smiled and nudged one another, knowing that we had pulled off a good one. The local newspaper music reviewer is perceptive and talented. He wrote: "*Messiah* is a musical gift that keeps on giving. It gave plenty in the Choral Society's performance!"

A personal moment of revelation occurred as we mixed with the audience after the concert. A newspaper columnist, whom I knew well as politically opposed and unfriendly to me in my election years, was in the audience and approached me with an astonished look saying, "Brooks, are you part of this?" His question seemed to have an edge and my political instincts kicked in at once. I wanted to reply, "Of course, you idiot, politicians have a soul and life outside election wars, and can sing, too!" But I just smiled and said, "Kate and I enjoy the Choral Society. Thanks for coming to the performance." As I later pondered the experience, I realized how far I had come from the partisan world of politics, and the cruelties of business economics, into a world of artistic involvement. A world that felt good and natural after years of career battles.

The success of that first concert with the Choral Society was a great impetus for Kate's and my early singing careers. As further evidence of that, after the second concert, on Sunday, we performed at our young grandson's birthday party. They had been to the concert and the family was celebrating in a local restaurant. Kate, in her long, formal dress, and I, in my black-tie tuxedo, snuck up behind nine-year-old Ben and sang a two-part harmony "Happy Birthday" at the top of our voices. The patrons cheered, and the family glowed. Even months previously, I never would have dared such a performance, but now I believed myself to be a singer.

* * *

Those of us in the retirement years are assaulted by behavioral scientific words such as "cognizance," "plasticity," "degeneration," "receptivity," and "congenital arrhythmia," that threaten and diminish our personal expectations. However, what I now know and live is that, at the age of sixty-nine, I was able to hold my own in the bass section of serious choral performances. The pure pleasure of that acquired singing ability is almost beyond description, and I love every minute of it. Don't confuse me with details; the Evensong time of life is full of potential.

Chapter Four

KATE DANCES

• • •

THE WORLD KNEW that Kate was intended to perform from the moment of her birth in Lebong, a small town in the mountain country of northeast India. Her mother, Lorna Boulton, began labor on the evening of a British community costume party. Her father, Walter, an Anglican priest, drove Lorna up to the hillside British Military Clinic only to find it dark and closed. He left her sitting on a bench outside and dashed back down to the party, returning rapidly with doctor and nurse. Unfortunately, the doctor had over-celebrated and was available only for consultation, so the nurse and Kate's mother did the job, and Kate joined the world. Kate's first view of her new circumstances was the doctor in clown face and costume and, most astonishingly, the nurse in ballet tutu! Her life pretty much continued as it began.

Kate's father was a Balliol Scholar at Oxford, and Lorna attended London University, unusual for a young woman at that time, and began her career as a teacher. She was pursuing this vocation in Calcutta, where she joined the Cathedral Choir and met the choir director, Walter Boulton. They were engaged six weeks later, but not married until they returned to England for a proper ceremony with Lorna's father, also an Anglican priest, officiating.

Those years were ideal for a young family in British colonial India, but the good life was interrupted by the Second World War. Walter had been assigned to be Bishop's Chaplain and acting Dean of the Cathedral in Calcutta, which allowed the family to live in a splendid house, shared with the bachelor bishop. Kate's first public performance was a tap dance— "When the Red, Red Robin Comes Bob, Bob, Bobbin' Along"—to entertain the lonely troops in Cathedral House: Toward the end of the war, the family returned to England and took up life in the home country. Postwar England was damp and dreary, and life was a cruel change from magical India.

Early on, young Kate had been spotted by dancing teachers for her limber athleticism and musicality. Back in England, in addition to a normal school curriculum, she worked at a ballet studio to improve her technique, although she would rather have played school sports. Her dancing teachers prepared her for a Royal Ballet School audition at the age of twelve, and she gained a rare acceptance; but her father would not allow her to attend a school that was primarily preparation for a stage career until she had passed her normal school matriculation. England has a national system of exams and, at the age of fourteen, Kate passed the English equivalency of United States high school.

Kate's early years in war-worn England were closer to a Jane Austen novel than contemporary life. The All Saint's Church vicarage in the Hampshire town of Fleet, where the Boultons settled, contained the Reverend, Mother, older sister Julia, younger brother John, and two younger sisters, Jane and Sarah, as well as a younger adopted sister Claudia. This menagerie lived a joyous, intellectual, and loving family life on ration books and a vicar's salary. Kate's parents were known to have solved both the *Times* and *Observer* crosswords by the end of Sunday tea time.

Some of Kate's distant memories are: longing for and then securing a second-hand bicycle; her father finally being given an antique car by an adoring parishioner; long, cold, bus rides down to her scholarship boarding school in Swanage, and more bus rides from there to ballet classes. They all lived in hand-me-down clothes and on short post-war rations. Sunday was the big day with a strict routine. Father presided over the early and then the ten o'clock services at All Saints Church, followed by a formal Sunday lunch in the dining room. Other days everyone ate in the kitchen, the warmest room in the house, with the laundry sometimes drying on a rack overhead. After lunch the routine provided for Father's sacred rest time and strict quiet in the house. Tea would be followed by Evensong at six, then supper and games.

Easter was an important time for the vicarage family because tradition determined that the parish collection plate would be a gift to the priest in charge, and also many good things delivered to the back door. Walter Boulton was very popular, and the family shouted in glee when a ham or box of candies came to grace the household. Kate remembers when they acquired an electric record player to replace the wind-up version in the drawing room. It was a usually cold and sometimes little-bit-hungry life, full of love and family. From this intellectually bright but modest vicarage household, sister Julia and brother John graduated from Cambridge, adopted sister Claudia graduated from Nottingham University, and sisters Jane and Sarah both went through London Acting Academies, all on scholarships. The young family members each went on to interesting careers and successful marriages, now with a crowd of children and grandchildren of their own. Kate grew up with the remote potential of a dancing career, the dream of many young English girls, but only a possibility with talent and intense, hard work.

At fourteen, Kate took a train to London with her ballet teacher and her mother to audition again for the Royal Ballet School, then called "Sadler's Wells." Only the best students were invited to appear, and on that day around fifty boys and girls nervously put on their black tops and pink or white tights in the dressing room for an audition class under the careful scrutiny of the ballet staff. Groups of eight were taken into the studio to perform with a piano accompanist. The students were first instructed to accomplish a stationary ballet bar warm-up, then slow adagio work in the center, and next, one by one, move across the floor, performing pirouettes and jetes, finishing as fast and as high as they could manage. Kate was talented with good flexibility and leg extension, and felt that she had done well, but the students were only given curt thank-you dismissals, and returned home, wondering. A week later, Kate's parents received a letter offering her a full scholarship to the Royal Ballet School.

She accepted, joined the upper school and began intense classes, this time with her father's blessing, and moved to London to share an apartment with other young girls. It is amazing to think of a fifteen-year-old Kate by herself in London, but the forties and fifties were a kinder and gentler time for young women on the streets of London. In time, individual upper school students were given minor roles in opera and ballet performances on the big stage of the Royal Opera House, a sign of progress and potential. An excited Kate spotted her first posting on the company bulletin board and phoned her parents to say that she had a part in the famous ballet, *The Sleeping Beauty*.

"What is it?" they asked.

"I'm a rat."

"A what? All this trouble for a rat?" her father grumbled.

Next year, at sixteen, she was invited to be a full member of the company and joined the Corps de Ballet.

In the world of choral singing, after audition acceptance, everyone becomes immersed in the music of the entire chorus and is rarely singled out to be evaluated individually. In the world of ballet, each daily class, as well as each rehearsal and performance, places a dancer under the watchful gaze of the ballet staff. The fearsome Royal Ballet director, Dame Ninette DeValois, the ballet mistress, the class directors, and choreographers watch and evaluate every move of their dancers, seeking talent and weeding out those prone to mistakes. Ballet classes, rehearsals, and performances are moments of startling beauty, but also have the subtle potential to put a career in jeopardy.

Perhaps the most romantically impressive vision on any stage is the opening of the second act of the *Swan Lake* ballet. To Tchaikovsky's symphonic violins, thirty-two princesses emerge from the stage wings in a dancing file to celebrate their nightly release from a spell that turned them into swans by day. The white-gowned dancers, spotlighted on a dark blue stage, must be in perfect unison, rhythm, and symmetry to enchant the audience with a rare moment of ethereal charm. Ballet moves may appear to be a simple exercise, but behind the romantic illusion is focus, concentration, and a daily life of work and dedication similar to that of an Olympic athlete. Each dancer must be perfectly aligned and exactly on tempo. Any deviation among the thirty-two might stand out and spoil the artistry, and very much be noticed. Beginning at age sixteen, Kate danced in that line many times, and later made three tours, enchanting audiences from New York across the country to California, traveling by ballet company train.

Kate was totally immersed in a serious career. The world of ballet dancing turns around daily technique classes and rehearsals. Health, fitness, physical training, and weight were daily concerns, as well as the competition among the dancers in the company and incredible pressure never to make a mistake or put a foot wrong on the stage. Behind every beautiful performance, and sylphlike beauty, lies daily grinding work and, often, a life of pain, always with a sore something. Constant staff review determines which dancers receive regular work, as well as the coveted solo roles, leading to artistic satisfaction, status, and pay increases.

As time went on, Kate toured the world and danced better roles. Her career took her outside London to the Netherlands, France, Belgium, Italy, Germany, and three tours of the United States and Canada. She became a solid member of the corps and also began to have solos.

One of Kate's strengths was the skill to learn dances easily and fit in quickly wherever she was needed. Once when on tour, she was down in the dressing room, putting on rich, tan Spanish makeup for the ballet of the evening, *Le Tricorne*. A frantic call came downstairs that a dancer was absent for "Les Sylphides," about to begin on stage. The staff found Kate, slapped on wet white makeup to cover the Spanish tan, zipped her into a white dress, and plonked a wreath on her head. She dashed on the stage just as the curtain rose, but nobody had told her which place she was to take. The opening pose was of sylphs in embracing groups, and she thought she saw an empty space. The blue lighting, white costumes, and powdery makeup on the dancers was dreamy, but, unfortunately, Kate stood out much darker in contrast, and especially in the bright lights. She tiptoed into a position she spotted in one group where an astonished dancer jumped back in alarm from the dusky foreigner and another whispered, "Not here, dear." She made up her role and danced in circles until, thankfully, with perspiration leaking the dark makeup through the white, she could plug into the spot of the missing dancer. Later, Madame De Valois, who terrified dancers even on a good day, saw Kate in the hall and chillingly remarked, "Thank you for filling in last night, Catherine, but do try to be in the right position next time."

On the American tour, the ballet company wound across the states in their own chartered train, and the lazy travel days were a welcome relief. The sunny country was appealing after gray London, and probably a factor in my future campaign to keep Kate here forever. She lectured a girls' school class in Texas about ballet and was gratified by their complete attention. When she finished, Kate asked if there were any questions. After a silence, one young lady raised her hand and said, "Where did y'all learn to talk like theyat?"

In Houston, they danced in a giant auditorium that was large enough to have two performance sides. Apparently there was a professional wrestling match going on in the second half, separated by many layers of thick curtains. Between acts, some of the dancers crept in the dark through the curtain screen to peek at the action. One of Kate's friends, who probably weighed ninety-five pounds wringing wet, and was gorgeous in stage makeup, tights, and tutu, took the lead. As she was peeking through the curtain a giant, hairy man in satin mask and cape sidled over to her and grunted, "Wanna wrestle?" There were squeals and shrieks as the sylphs retreated back through the drapes.

The star of the ballet for many years was the inimitable Margot Fonteyn, one of the most famous dancers of all time, but also a down-to-earth, decent person. Kate's most important role was as the second lead, the "Lilac Fairy" to Fonteyn's "Princess Aurora" in *The Sleeping Beauty*. Kate's part involved much acting and mime, which she enjoyed and did well, but the solo dancing involved always meant a good deal of pressure. Kate's future husband enjoyed watching her dance this part in Los Angeles where she appeared in the role for the first time with her tour roommate, the gorgeous Anya Linden, destined to be a lifelong friend, in the lead role. Anya went on to become a famous ballerina before marrying John Sainsbury; they later became Lord and Lady Sainsbury. However, Kate was destined to fall under the spell of California, leaving to be married sooner in her career than Anya.

Kate lived and breathed the romantic ballet world, spreading magic from the concert stage. Life was exhausting but glamorous, performing with good friends, and seeing the world with the company. There was also an element of down-to-earth friendliness and support in the ballet company. In one performance, the famous Margot Fonteyn, circling the stage with energetic turns, slipped and fell on her backside. As she swiftly jumped to her feet, she grimaced at the ring of startled dancers on the stage and exclaimed, "Ouch, my bum is numb!" Such is the glamorous world of ballet. In another performance, the choreography called for twelve princesses to toss soft magic oranges back and forth to each other while dancing. On opening night, everything went wrong and the stage was strewn with balls. A reviewer in the London press remarked that the "Royal Ballet cricket club was not ready for a match!" Kate was put out by this because, with her earlier school sports training, she managed to be the only one left holding a ball at the end of the dance. She proved her catching skills again in another ballet, *Giselle*. The heroine threw away a pearl necklace given her by the princess, and Kate made an unscripted catch of the jewels, only to toss them hastily away backstage.

Another performance near the end of an exhausting tour on the road, *The Firebird*, called for an evil sorcerer to enchant the castle and dance everyone into hypnotized sleep. Once again, Kate was one of twelve maidens that the sorcerer forced to dance rapidly, then dazedly, as the music slowed, with the dancers weaving back and forth and, finally, collapsing on the stage. As the lights dimmed, the final movement was to roll over, pause, and then slowly roll back and pause again. The music and action became softer and slower. On the return roll, only eleven princesses made the move, because Kate was sound asleep!

This was Kate's tight world of friends and ballet discipline, but at the conclusion of a routine performance in New York, during Kate's second tour of America in 1956, life changed. We met and were married two years later, after her third tour. Our fifty-three years have taken us through many chapters to our present state of retirement in California. There is no doubt that our many years of family and career life have brought maturity and alterations to our outlooks, appearance, and way of life, but there has been very little change in our fundamentals or basic characters. We still appear to each other, and our families and close friends, very much the same as when we were married.

Some years later, her ballet companion Anya Linden, now re-tired and with children of her own, visited us at our cattle ranch in California. Anya wanted to join us in a roundup, and as she was a somewhat tenuous rider, I put a halter and rope on a very calm mount and we set out with me leading her while I rode my reliable ranch horse. The two of us followed the crew, including Kate, our three teenagers, neighbors, and ranch hands, who all were part of the large herd gathering. At one moment, Kate was trying to push some steers off an oak-covered hill and Anya and I were on a ridge, directly opposite, a hundred yards away, with a steep canyon between us. We could not see her because of the oak trees, but we could hear Kate clearly having a tough time. With Anya on a lead rope there was nothing I could do to help, and could only await events. We heard rustling up and down the oak hill, then the usual, "Hyah!" to get the cattle moving There was another, louder, "Hyah! Hyah!" and we could sense a more urgent scurrying behind the trees on the opposite hillside. Finally, there was a, "Get out of there you #$%^&!" Then in a different spot, "Move on you #$%^&*!" Anya gave me a glance. Then we heard again, "Hyeaah! You #$%^&* cattle!" This time, Anya turned to me and said, "My! Kate has changed." I replied, "No, I don't think she will ever change."

We have raised four children—now all married, and have thirteen grandchildren. We spent four years in England during my Firestone Tire career and then moved to the cattle ranch and winery for most of our married life. Kate endured a number of political campaigns and, in one of them, had a face-to-face confrontation with my opponent until aides nervously whisked her away. Once she had a delightful and unusually long chat with the Queen of England, who was visiting Los Angeles on the Royal Yacht, while local bigwigs impatiently awaited their turn for an audience. Another year she acted the part of Mrs. Graves in the play *Enchanted April*, and astonished the locals by taking to it naturally. While on a winery tour, she won the grand prize for cooking at a March of Dimes "Celebrity Chef Cook-Off." She is tireless, determined, and really more from a previous age rather than our modern time. She is who she is and people are fascinated by her, but I get to live with her.

Many years ago, while raising our young family in Monterey, California, a local music teacher encouraged Kate to sing in the Carmel Bach Festival. Kate could sing naturally and early piano lessons had given her the ability to read music. After passing the audition, she sang in the chorus of *St. Mathew Passion* with Maestro Sandor Salgo conducting. This and the local St. Mark's Choir was all there was of her singing career, until we both discovered the joys of serious choral music. It had never occurred to her to pursue music further, but when her husband started taking lessons, she joined in the new avocation happily. Her audition with the Santa Barbara Choral Society went well, and we found ourselves looking across at each other in rehearsal from bass to alto sections. After a busy lifetime of the ups and downs of aching ballet muscles, raising a large family, numerous house moves, business careers, ranching chores, political battles, and growing up together in married life, we account ourselves incredibly lucky to be singing together in our kinder, gentler, but still challenging life.

Chapter Five

ABOUT SINGING

● ● ●

THE LARGEST TRAIL-riding organization in the country, and probably the world, is called "Rancheros Visitadores." This group of around a thousand members, adhering to western traditions, gather with their horses once a year for a week of camping out in the hills of California.

Before the annual trek, in a year after I had sung a few seasons with the Choral Society, I joined about a dozen fellow Rancheros, who had arrived in camp a day early, around a large campfire, consuming whiskey under the stars. Western singing is very much part of the tradition, so three accomplished players were strumming their guitars and had brought song sheets so we could all join in. We were pals, and very happy in our music.

Music is very much a part of the old west and has entertained cowboys around campfires for generations. During cattle-trail drives, cowboys on night duty would slowly ride in circles around the bedded-down animals, singing. Large groups of cattle in strange settings can be spooked by night sounds, and the resulting stampede could scatter injured animals for miles. To offset alarming sounds breaking into a peaceful night, such as a mountain lion chuffing, a bear groaning, or a coyote howling, the singing cowboys would calm the herd. There was probably a very mixed quality of performances from those grizzled characters, but as long as they maintained some steady noise they were accomplishing their job. Our campfire music that night was on the upper end of cowboy tradition, and if there had been a herd of critters nearby, they probably would have remained peaceful and dozy.

One of my pals said, "Brooks, we know you've been singing up a storm with that fancy chorus. Why don't you give us one of your songs?" And that was the last thing I wanted to do because, as much as I enjoy singing in a group, I dreaded solos. But the gang persisted and I ran out of excuses.

"Okay," I said, "here's a piece we sang in St. Peter's, at the Vatican. It's meant to be sung by a choir and has been around a few centuries. It's in Latin and, roughly translated, says that where love is, there is God also." The group was sympathetic to the religious theme and settled in to listen.

I had some whiskey courage, which seemed to help my performance, particularly with the low notes. Singers understand that sometimes, for reasons unknown, their voice is better than other times. I nailed it, including a low E that I can rarely negotiate with volume. That night my solo came off as well as any I ever attempted. I sang: *"Ubi caritas et amor, Deus ibi est. Ubi caritas et amor, Deus ibi est. Congregavit, nos in unum Christi amor. Congregavit, nos in unum Christi amor..."*

There was a stunned silence around the campfire as I sat down and, finally, a murmur of general approval as we picked up more western songs. About a year later I asked one of my friends to tell me straight what kind of reaction there was to my solo, as I did not know what the group had felt. He replied that no one had wanted to speak because they were all very moved and emotional.

Another group of wonderful singers, and certainly among the most enthusiastic, are in "barbershop" groups. There are many organizations throughout the country, and in Britain, with more than 25,000 men, and another 25,000 women, many of whom belong to the "Sweet Adelines" organization. These groups welcome new people, both men and women, and help them join in the singing. Somehow, I have never participated in a barbershop group, which is why this dimension of music is not featured. But for anyone interested in singing, either as part of an audience or a participant, a barbershop club is a most enjoyable musical experience.

There is a wide world of music, and the ability to express group friendship, inspire emotions, calm cattle, and sing at the Vatican are only parts. Chorus America, which is the very able organization promoting choral singing, estimates that there are about 270,000 singing groups of all kinds in the United States. Of these, 12,000 are community choruses of varying background and expertise, 41,000 are school choruses, and 216,000 are church choirs. Over forty million people, young and old, sing in some kind of organized group in our country.

There is much speculation about future interest in choral singing, including some positive signs. Vocal group competitions are popular television shows, and the series *Glee*, based on a high school singing group, is currently in its third season. A television drama series, successful in England and America, called *The Choir*, features a young conductor, Gareth Malone, teaching a good portion of a town to sing in a large chorus. Both President Obama, crooning an Al Green song into the microphone, and candidate

Mitt Romney vocalizing "Oh, beautiful for spacious skies, for amber waves of grain..." on the campaign trail confirm that real men sing. Most of all, choral singing, as shown in the adventures described in these chapters, is too much fun not to continue as a major element in the culture of our country.

Anyone can sing on the most basic level, from children's lullabies to bar room ballads. Just like tasting wine, one can enjoy a casual slurp, or make a lifelong study of vintages and vintners. Vocal cords can be fine-tuned, and flavor discerning palates can develop sophistication for greater enjoyment, rather than merely letting nature take its course. There should be no intimidation about studying music, and even a little knowledge is a good thing.

Our son, Andrew, was recruited by ABC Television for the popular series, *The Bachelor*. This famous reality show ran for eight weeks, during which one eligible young man had to choose a potential bride from twenty-five even more eligible young ladies, through a process of elimination symbolized by presenting roses to those who were to stay on the show. One would think the program would be a great pleasure for the man, surrounded by so many lovelies, but the stress of presenting roses to a diminishing cast of hopefuls, and ultimately choosing the most likely, proved to be nervous agony to Andrew over the course of the show. He had a lifetime experience and carried off the challenge with style and charm; but, alas, none of the interesting young women won his heart.

At one moment during the filming, he surprised a group of otherwise accomplished beauties attempting to sing a song. Unfortunately, it was not an impressive experience and did nothing to enhance the prospects of the bachelorettes. Throughout history, love and courtship have abounded with memorable ballads, but these modern bachelorettes, like too many of their contemporaries, had somehow missed the opportunity to learn the musical basics that might otherwise have fostered a liaison. If for no other reason than improving romantic potential, a little music coaching must be a good thing. Perhaps Andrew's heart could have been won by a song, but the show is long gone, and he is now happily married and we have an infinitely rewarding daughter-in-law (not part of the show), and two equally rewarding grandchildren.

Singing is a combination of musical knowledge and vocal technique. Basic music understanding can be something of an uphill push, like learning a foreign language. There are whole notes and sixteenth notes and everything in between. There are clefs and sharps and flats and measures and scales and...on and on. The basics may come faster or may come slower, but learning takes time and sweat. Brilliant minds learn quickly, and slower minds, like mine, take time; but the moment will come when the mysteries are revealed, and a music page will be a friendly script allowing one to plunk out the notes to be sung with the appropriate rhythm. That moment is a joy.

Next, beyond technical musical skills, the voice needs training, regardless of natural tone, and here a helpful teacher is indispensable in acquiring good vocal skills. Breathing is critically important, and one must learn about the diaphragm and deep, lower breathing as opposed to a shallow, panting breath. Positions of the throat, tongue, mouth, and the use of vocal chords as instruments sounded by the wind of breath all interact to produce a shaped note. Many small nuances build upon natural talents, and soon an acceptable, and sometimes a surprising tone, will emerge. Of course there are always those who will not be mathematicians or tightrope walkers or singers, but almost anyone can learn to improve with vocal instruction. In the normal course of events, musical knowledge, rhythm, pitch, and tone will provide the substance for a singing voice, and then the fun begins.

Beyond the group song sheets, happy birthdays, or communal

participation in hymns and national anthems, there are the pleasures of choir singing and the adventures of choral performances such as Kate and I have enjoyed. Our St. Mark's choir is typical of a volunteer group of church friends who sing the service and anthem on most Sundays. Our routine is to arrive at 8:30 a.m., before the 10:00 service, and warm up with the congregational hymns to be sung before tackling the anthem. Our director, the ever-pleasant and delightfully insisting Rose Knoles, who also plays the church organ and piano, will have chosen a piece of music that often appears impossible, but will gradually unravel and emerge into a presentable piece of music to be sung for the congregation. We are appreciated as volunteer friends and neighbors who work hard to contribute to the worship service. The choir is a congregation within the congregation. We are proud of what we do, and know that when we sing well, we enhance the liturgy with musical expressions of praise, prayer, contrition, thanksgiving, wonder, and all the dimensions of communal worship. We delight in our successes, cringe at our mistakes, and always try our best.

Our other group is the Santa Barbara Choral Society, representative of a large, talented volunteer organization singing serious vocal music. Kate and I are lucky to sing with the hundred members who work hard to achieve a high standard, and are blessed with an excellent director, Jo Anne Wasserman. Each season we will sing at least once with the Santa Barbara Symphony, perform two other formal concerts, and seek out less formal events as the opportunity arises. Every two or three years we will organize an overseas trip, which have all been great successes. As most singing groups, the Society is a congenial, eclectic conglomeration, with all the social dynamics of many people working together. Finances and fundraising are always a problem, particularly in these difficult economic times.

Jo Anne demands and receives our best, which is never good

enough. We are blessed with a first-class accompanist, David Potter, who reads Jo Anne's mind and always begins at the right place in the music at the right tempo. Sometimes, in rehearsals, seated members (and more often than not the bass section) will fail to hear instructions and might suffer from attention deficit disorder; but, by and large, there is intense effort and a desire to improve. We enjoy our professional section leaders who set the tone and pace and help guide their neighbors, particularly in the early period of learning a difficult piece.

The Society is always short of tenors, and some of us think their scarcity value spoils them. The basses like to flirt with the sopranos who like to flirt with the tenors. Basses marry altos, who hold the chorus together both with voice and organizational skills. We know who in the Society will be late for rehearsals and who will struggle in the learning phases of a piece. We know the people we like to sit next to for rehearsals because they have the best voices, and we know who we like to have a beer with after, and they are not necessarily the same person. The audience perceives a unified and disciplined whole making beautiful music. The fact is we are people with quirks and individualities and all the squirrelly dramas that accompany artistic group dynamics.

The chorus depends on Jo Anne and we hang on her every move during rehearsal and concert. If she were to sneeze on the podium, we would probably all sing, "God bless you." During one concert, she turned two pages at once in a place where the soloist was just finishing and the soprano section was coming in. There was a moment of panic when signals were truly crossed: the orchestra carrying on, the soloist waiting for cut-off, and the ladies waiting for an entrance cue. In the minds of the chorus there was alarm, but only for a measure, then all came back together. After the performance we learned that no one in the audience had noticed our panic. It is amazing that there are very few mistakes in the complicated and fast-moving pieces of music, and that, when they happen, we remember every detail. We all work diligently to maintain a professional standard.

Our church choir and choir society strive to be the best possible, and both groups rehearse and work hard to accomplish a memorable and inspirational sound. Each member will never be good enough in their own minds. Kate and I are amazed that we are so deeply involved and dedicated to the singing world; but it is a passion in our lives and we will continue as long as we are able.

Chapter Six

THINGS EPISCOPAL

• • •

KATE AND I HAVE ALWAYS been Anglican/Episcopalian, and are very much involved in the church and recommend that others be included also. We both enjoy attending our local St. Mark's and visits to Anglican/Episcopal churches around the world to experience the local interpretations and variations of worship.

A popular misconception is that the Anglican/Episcopal church began at the whim of King Henry the Eighth to satisfy his greed and lust. The truth is far more complicated and inspirational. In the turbulent 1500s, the movement for independence, which had always been lurking in the souls of English Christians, merged with the European Reformation led by Martin Luther, John Calvin, and others to seek Church reform, or separation from Rome.

These upheavals ultimately led to the dissolution of the English from the central authority of the Roman Church and brought into being the independent Anglican Church. Conforming to details of theology was more crucial to the church in the 1500s than today, and clergy and laypeople were prepared to die in the most cruel ways rather than betray their convictions. A marker in front of Balliol College, in the heart of downtown Oxford, shows the place where Bishops Cranmer, Latimer, and Ridley were tied to a stake and burnt for their belief in a more accessible and self-governing Anglican church. Archbishop Cranmer, author of the revised *Prayer Book*, including the Evensong service, and his fellow bishops, were not the only ones to die for their beliefs.

In 1906, my great-grandfather on my mother's side of the family, William Elroy Curtis, wrote a journal titled, "A Pilgrim's Peregrinations in the Land of His Forefathers." On his travels through England he unearthed the transcript of the trial of our Curtis ancestor, Roger Coo, an English layman who held strong Anglican convictions and, consequently, was burnt around the same time as Ridley, Latimer, and Cranmer. Somehow, Coo came to the attention of the Roman Catholic authorities in the reign of the fierce Catholic, Queen Mary. Roger Coo was examined by a local bishop in 1555; following is the sad conclusion of the actual transcript:

"Thus Roger Coo, an aged father, after his sondry troubles and conflicts with his adversaries, at length was committed to the fire at Yexford in the County of Suffolke, where he most blessedly ended his aged years. Anno 1555, Mens. Septemb."

The "blood of the martyrs" flows in my veins and probably also in Kate's with her clerical forebears. My ancestor was burnt to death for his testimony, and I sigh with sadness for him and the bickering that made disputed church doctrine lethal among otherwise Christian believers. We all shudder when contemplating the past, and trust that our present security and freedoms will not place us in mortal jeopardy for the fine points of our convictions.

However, despite the dark early days, the Anglican Church survived and prospered and introduced the church to the new world.

The present-day Episcopal Church emerges from a rich and dramatic history of religion in America. The French and Spanish Roman Catholics brought Christianity to the wilds of the Midwest and the settlements of Florida. The reformed Puritans, or Congregationalists, settled in Massachusetts, and, from there, free thinkers escaped to settle in Rhode Island. The Quakers established themselves in Philadelphia, the Dutch Reformed Calvinists moved into New Amsterdam, now New York, and the Scandinavian Lutherans settled in the Delaware Valley and, later, thrived in the northern plains. The Presbyterians and Methodists won converts and established churches throughout the Colonies, and the Unitarians prospered as a reaction to the stricter denominations.

The Anglican Church had a strong presence throughout the colonies, but with a growing problem because, in England, Anglicans were the established state religion with the king as head of the Church as well as the country. As time went on, a mounting desire for independence soon brought the Anglican Church into a difficult position. Things English became unfashionable with a growing bitterness in the colonies toward the home country.

By the 1770s, the American Colonies were seething with the growing pains of a country ready for independence. The "Rebels" made the most noise, but, in fact, only about a third of the populace preferred independence from Great Britain; about a third did not care one way or another, and a third were Royalists who wanted to remain in the British Empire. The Church of England, such as it was in America amongst the competing denominations, appeared to favor the Royalists. After all, Anglicanism was then the official Church of England with the king as the head of the church, to whom all priests swore allegiance.

Hurtful words were exchanged. The Reverend Samuel Seaury,

later to become the first Episcopal bishop, wrote to Alexander Hamilton, "Consider, Sir, is it right to risk the valuable blessings of property, liberty and life, to the single chance of war? Of the worst kind of war—a civil war? a civil war founded on rebellion?" However, despite the obvious stigma of the Anglican Church favoring the king over the Revolution, the records show that around two-thirds of the signers of the Declaration of Independence, and two-thirds of the signers of the Constitution were Anglicans. George Washington himself was a member of the Church of England. But when the Royalists ultimately lost, the priests and congregations, who identified with the losing English side, and who did not go into exile to Canada or England, remained in an awkward position.

However, the former Anglican Church survived, independent of the Church of England, and with the new name, "Episcopal." The Anglican philosophy, theology, and liturgy remained in a new self-governing denomination, and soon the American Episcopal Church became a leading denomination in America, and one of the separate and equal members of the Anglican Communion. The Episcopal Church grew and headed west with the growing United States. In 2012 there are around two million souls attending Episcopal Churches on Sunday, and many more claiming membership, but rarely going to services. The sixties showed a steep decline in attendance, but recently membership seems to be holding.

Liturgical history has been most kind because, through all the many years of Anglican/Episcopal Church upheavals and travails, Thomas Cranmer's words and spirit remain essentially as written in the blessed *Book of Common Prayer*. The substance of the Prayer Book litany has survived and prevailed, aided by the breadth of wording, perhaps sometimes ambiguous to the congregation, and open to broad interpretation by intellectuals, but beautiful and inspirational to the populace. The High Church Anglo Catholics and Low Church Evangelicals all have found comfort in their understanding of the *Book of Common Prayer* and its services. Most importantly, congregations with less enthusiasm for intellectual trends have loved their service book as it is, and without alteration. And, above all, to this Episcopalian, the Evening Prayer Service, or what is known to many as "Evensong," has survived very much intact.

As I have said, in 1958 Kate and I were married in Holy Trinity, Guildford, by Kate's Father, the dean. Leaving nothing to chance, I arrived at the church early, before the service and was met with a clamorous peal of bells ringing in the tower. I peered behind a curtain to discover six men absorbed in their task, counting strange rhythms aloud while tugging ropes that lifted them into the air. They continued steadily for forty-five minutes, and I later discovered that they were pealing a carillon that had been written specially for the wedding. I also noticed a large crowd collecting on the High Street outside the steps to the church. The local paper, the *Surrey Advertiser*, had written headlines saying, "Dean to Marry Ballet Dancer!"

The wedding service in the large church with our families and friends is still vivid in both our minds. In the English ceremony, instead of the wedding march as the bride processes, the congregation sings a hymn. I still remember trying to choke out, "Now Thank We All Our God" as the beautiful Kate processed the long aisle on the arm of her brother, and under the officiating eye of her father. The Very Reverend Walter Boulton presented a formidable demeanor to this young California man who was stealing his daughter. He performed the ceremony with joy and finality, and I knew we were truly married when we walked back down the aisle into the sunlight and through the cheering crowd to our coach-like car and driver.

I am sure her English friends wondered about this California youth; and my family and friends who made the trip must have wondered if I knew what I was doing in England. Kate and I are still in wonder. We are both happy in the Episcopal Church. The combination of historical legitimacy, intellectual honesty, openness, and worshipful presence fills our definition of the place where we want to worship. As stated before, we recommend the church to all.

Chapter Seven

Community Voices

• • •

COUNTRIES, CULTURES, AND CIVILIZATIONS
are built and defined by people. For instance, we enjoy the great
historic cathedrals in Europe today because people decided to
build them in the Middle Ages. Other countries have little or
nothing because, over the generations, other people lacked inspiration and organization to build and maintain a meaningful culture and infrastructure to ensure continuity. To our great, local,
good fortune, in 1997 a group of Santa Barbarans joined together
and acquired a large downtown movie theater of the grand '40s
era, called the "Granada," with a determination to construct a performing arts center.

The financial contributions, talent, and hard work needed to
transform the Granada from films to live performances were a testimony to the energy of our town, its vision, and personal com-

mitment. A leading citizen, Michael Towbes, accepted the call to be chair of the committee with inspiration and dedication. One person donated ten million dollars, five people donated five to ten million, four donated one to five million, seven donated five hundred thousand to a million, and countless others contributed according to their abilities. In addition there were auctions, events, and fundraising schemes of every nature, with most of the town joining in. Ten years of energetic and competent management, faith, perseverance, and all the best instincts of a great community produced the Granada ready for the grand opening in March 2008.

To celebrate the gala first-night performance, the Granada Board decided to invite an array of artistic groups to represent the type of events that could now utilize the new theater. The resident local companies—Santa Barbara Symphony, Opera Santa Barbara, State Street Ballet, and the Santa Barbara Choral Society—were all to feature preview performances, showing their best sample of upcoming Granada entertainment. Tickets would be sold at fundraising prices, and the gala evening would be the event of the year in our town.

On the big night, people bought the expensive seats and turned out in full formal dress, filling the house with glitter and glamour. The sellout crowd was excited and proud of the Granada because almost everyone in Santa Barbara had a stake in the project. As the crowd strolled through the red-curtained, freshly painted, and gold-trimmed lobby there was a buzz of excitement. The evening was everything the founders had dreamed of through the years.

At the time, the Choral Society was rehearsing for a grand and impactful choral work, *Carmina Burana*, a modern piece by Carl Orff, to be presented later in the year together with the State Street Ballet dancing a dramatic original ballet. For the gala Granada night, we decided to sing the opening chorus, without dancers, accompanied by the Santa Barbara Symphony. The modern and brash music in *Carmina* is full of sound and drama, and we were to discover and enjoy just how dramatic. The work, when performed by a large chorus, is always popular and begins with a familiar phrase. The Latin words may or may not be well known, but when heard with the music are instantly recognizable from films, advertisements, and dramas of all kinds. The score begins with a double forte, which is choral license to soar, and the Latin words add to the impact: *"O fortuna... vel ut luna... sta tu vari abilis!"* or, "Oh Fortune, like the moon, you are always changing!" The volume then dampens to a quiet double piano, which is just as well because our voices could not maintain the starting RPMs.

On the big night, after the crowd settled, and when the lights faded, there were the inevitable speeches followed by various performances. Of course, each organization presented their best, and the audience responded with cheers. Our part of the program was in the second half, and we found that we were very fortunate in our placement.

The Santa Barbara Symphony Orchestra playing for us that night was filled with the maximum number of musicians, and our Society Chorus was also in force with some additional "ringers" who wanted to come along for the occasion. During our backstage lineup, for once, there were no whispered words, and the Symphony and Chorus mood was quiet determination. We all crowded to our places behind the curtain in careful silence and stood patiently, waiting to explode.

Our chorus was preceded by two local prodigies who played piano and violin, performing a soft and melodic piece. There had been a long, champagne-graced intermission, and some of my friends in the audience said the theater mood was a little dozy after an exciting first half. The innocent audience enjoying the duet did not realize that coiled to strike behind the silent curtain was

a symphony orchestra, and more than a hundred singers standing on risers—both formidable weapons. Orchestra and chorus
focused in total silence, more than ready for the job ahead. We
could all feel the moment and were in a mood to go for it, fully
understanding the potential impact of the opening piece.

Our conductor, Jo Anne Wasserman, took her place at the podium, ready when the curtain quietly rose to reveal the mass of musicians. At that moment, there was an instant silence as performers and audience faced off. The downbeat of *Carmina Burana* is a
full orchestra chord, punctuated by an oversized bass drum, and
the next note adds a full voiced, double forte, crashing, "O!" My
friends out front told me later that the audience literally jumped
out of their seats on our opening shock. The bass voices played off
the drum with a firm and lusty foundation; the tenors, as usual
when given license, soared; the altos unfurled their full, feminine
wings and richly nurtured and bonded the mix; the sopranos, as
is their wont, sailed to the ceiling and rained magic; and the symphony played their hearts out. When we all came down to earth
again with the quiet section, Kate and I—and I am sure the whole
chorus—were in a chill of excitement.

All the musicians felt a bonding with the audience, and we
responded to their presence as much as possible in a big performance. The audience brought joy and sense of accomplishment in
the realization of a major ten-year project. The performers echoed
that emotion with the extraordinary pleasure of the first night's
appearance in the new Granada, and presented their liveliest and
best. On finishing, the singers beamed breathlessly and the orchestra smiled while the audience gave us a standing cheer.

Of course, all the performances were splendid: symphony, ballet, opera, Spanish dancers, soloists and others were at their best.
But somehow, and in all modesty, I believe the takeaway moment
was the symphony and chorus explosion of *Carmina Burana*.

The Choral Society members were aglow with the warmth of local singers participating in a community event that celebrated our Santa Barbara Granada Performing Arts Center. The night was a rare experience of communal exuberance and joy.

The following year, the Choral Society had an opportunity to thank Michael Towbes, Granada Chair and inspiration of the project. A splendid birthday party was given him by friends, family, and community. In order to recognize his accomplishments in a meaningful way, the party was organized as a fundraiser for his beloved Granada for about eight hundred people in the outdoor Red Lion Hotel Rotunda. When the cake was brought in, the Society Chorus paraded behind, and joyfully led the assemblage in a four part "Happy Birthday" that rose to the skies in the open space. Kate and I felt grateful to be performers on both occasions that meant so much to Santa Barbara.

* * *

On another, very different, occasion, the choral community joined to express grief and sorrow in an historical tragedy, a monstrous event in town that had moved the populace to shock and grief. On an otherwise quiet night, a deranged former employee somehow entered the Goleta Postal Sorting Facility and shot to death seven innocent employees and then killed herself.

The local population, the postal workers, and all the first responders from law enforcement, emergency medical response, and postal agencies were grieved and outraged. The husbands, wives, children, and families of the victims were overcome with sadness and horror. For many days after, the only issue discussed in the neighborhoods and media was this terrible tragedy. A popular notion welled up to hold a commemorative event to express the feelings of the local community and share our common grief and sympathy for the families of the victims. Accordingly, a committee was formed to devise a plan for a suitable ceremony.

I became involved because I had been elected County Supervisor in 2004. Local politics is every bit as contentious and partisan as national elections; nevertheless, Kate and I suspended normal life and campaigned for supervisor successfully, but not without a tough election. Neither of us enjoyed the exposure that came with political life and we would be hard put to explain why we wanted to be so deeply involved. My politics tend to be slightly right of center which means that I take hits from both ends of the spectrum. The five Santa Barbara County Supervisors deal with everything from potholes to budgets, including community events, and that brought me to the tragedy in 2006.

The incident took place in the city of Goleta, just north of Santa Barbara, but the city mayor was preoccupied with a legal problem and unable to involve herself in planning the event. Although she was politically left of center and I was on the right, we worked well together. She asked me, as the supervisor for the area, to chair the organizing committee and devise a memorial service as soon as possible. The Federal Postal Service spared no effort in counseling the families, and were initially opposed to any public exposure for them. However, after lengthy discussions with the committee and consultation with the professionals helping the devastated families, the Washington officials agreed that, if planned correctly, a community ceremony would be a positive. Thus began a series of intense meetings and planning sessions, which I chaired, to come up with an event that would be good both for the families of the victims and the community.

These occasions often involve repetitive speakers, usually politicians wanting to be sincere, but also seeking public exposure and publicity, and the ceremonies drag on at length in sentimental fulminations. We tried not to let this be part of our event. The University of California Santa Barbara, not far from the Post Office facility agreed to open their six-thousand-seat basketball stadium, the Thunderdome, for the occasion. The committee determined there would be only six speakers and each would deliver a specific message. The ceremony would be closely timed, with nothing left to chance. It would be a community outpouring of sympathy and grief for the surviving families, both a religious and non-religious ceremony, with no sponsor or authority beyond the committee and generosity of the university.

The specifics were devised to span the many emotions and points of view surrounding the occasion, and we accomplished this in rapid time, scheduled for only two weeks after the tragedy. Happily, the unique circumstances and press of time eliminated all the usual nonsense of open public meetings and interminable discussions. We had complete authority to get on and do the job. Only speeches from the Goleta mayor, the county sheriff, the university chancellor, the county religious convocation chair, the United States postmaster general, and a blessing from the presiding Catholic cleric would be on the program. I carefully excluded myself from speaking, which helped me resist the requests of other officials and politicians.

I did not speak, but I did sing.

Not every committee of this nature is chaired by a choral singer, but this one was and we proceeded accordingly. We decided to make choral singing an important part of the service, and we put out a call to every singing organization in the county to participate. The response was incredible, both in quantity and quality, with the community College Chorus Director, Nathan Kreitzer, agreeing to conduct.

We did not know ahead of time who would show up to sing. However, we received positive replies from the following organizations: Alan Hancock College Singers, Dos Pueblos High School chorus; the choirs of the El Montecito Presbyterian, First United Methodist, St. Mark's Episcopal, Trinity Lutheran, Lompoc Master Chorale, San Marcos High School Chorus, Santa Barbara Choral Society, Santa Ynez Chorale, Santa Barbara City College Music Department, Santa Barbara Master Chorale, University of California Santa Barbara, and Westmont College. Additionally, a number of individual singers volunteered. On the day of the service more than two-hundred-and-fifty voices, divided into soprano, alto, tenor, and bass sections, occupied the Thunderdome bleachers behind the speaker's stand.

Singers were asked to arrive an hour early, and Nathan Kreitzer led a very hasty forty-five minute rehearsal with a piano brought in for the occasion. We sang "America the Beautiful," the "23rd Psalm" set to "Brother James's Air," a beautiful and inspiring anthem, "There Shall Be Rest," and concluded the service with "Amazing Grace." It became immediately obvious in rehearsal that we had a beautiful sound from the massed singers with the Thunderdome acoustics.

The event proceeded smoothly, and on schedule, with about three thousand attendees. While we sang, the families were ushered in and out with dignity from a side room, surrounded and shepherded by postal department officials, with no media allowed. The large space was completely quiet throughout the ceremony and there were few dry eyes in the assembled crowd. The speakers were sincere, spoke to their script, and the agenda went off without a problem. When the families came forward one by one to receive their recognition, the Thunderdome was charged with emotion.

The choral music added to the meaning and healing of the event. The impromptu crowd of voices sang beautifully and filled the large space with a sound that reflected the feelings and sympathies of the assembled community perfectly, and in a way the spoken word could not completely accomplish. The families of the victims and people attending knew that this was an assembly of local singers who desired to add to the ceremony with true community expression.

If a large public gathering on such a tragic occasion can be called a success, it was. Everyone associated with the memorial expressed a sense that it had been done correctly, and brought closure and pride to the community. The postal authorities were pleased that the locals had responded in such an appropriate fashion to the tragedy. To my mind, however, the best compliment came from a tough sheriff's captain who was in on all the organizing meetings and concerned with traffic, crowd control, and security. He came up to me in the after-ceremony quiet and said, "You know, I didn't get that singing stuff when it was planned, but it was good. It was good."

A community with a tradition and organized talent to sing offers a positive dimension and enhanced life for all. The Santa Barbara area is fortunate that there is a communal desire to maintain choral music and that there is the available talent to perform. May it always be so.

Chapter Eight

BUSINESS AND BEAUTY

• • •

SHAKESPEARE IN LOVE is an amusing and well-made film about the circumstances that might have surrounded the production of *Romeo and Juliet*. The film relates the economic vicissitudes of the Globe Theater trying to produce Shakespeare's masterpiece and is a great romp in the Elizabethan world. The historic theater was continually threatened by bankruptcy, and the remote prospect of underwriting the play is referred to in the film as a "miracle." The Santa Barbara Choral Society has functioned for sixty-four years, and the very existence of the organization, as well as the financial problems of mounting major choral productions, is also a history of such financial miracles.

Somehow, choral music does not come to the top of donor lists and, even with small budgets, compared to other types of performing organizations, endures an ongoing struggle for funding.

The Society has normal operating costs including music director, accompanist, section leaders, rehearsal hall, and management overhead, all of which are a challenge to fund in themselves. Additionally, the cost of producing a major choral performance with orchestra, soloists, venue, publicity, and all the other incidental expenses, is only partially covered by ticket revenue, adding to the Society's total burden. Foundations, sponsors, patrons, and community donors are the life blood of our existence and our productions, and, since the onset of recession beginning in 2008, donor largess has become a scarce commodity. The Society, a non-profit corporation, elects a board of directors to wrestle with the financial realities of our organization and all singers help in funding as they are able.

Nearly a year before our 2011 winter/spring concert season, the Santa Barbara Choral Society Board faced the decision of what to sing and where. Our artistic ambition was to undertake an important work, and possibly the most beautiful choral work of all time, J.S. Bach's *B Minor Mass*. However, economic factors weighed in heavily, and technical alternatives and financial factors were debated extensively because this was a major piece of music requiring an orchestra. The business of the production loomed large against the beauty of performing this incredible work for the community and for our own artistic fulfillment. Finally, after adopting a tough budget, we gulped, undertook the challenge, and decided to sing the *B Minor Mass*. Our program decision was a victory for beauty over business realities.

Our first production decision for the performance, to abandon the venue of Santa Barbara's splendid Granada Performing Arts Center, was difficult, but considerations of added theater costs and the problem of filling the fifteen-hundred seats led us to a smaller concert site, the San Roque Catholic Church. Acoustics were excellent in the six-hundred-seat church, the costs were well below the Granada expenses, and the church was pleased to host the concert. Our very accomplished piano and organ accompanist, David Potter, also the music director and a member of San Roque Church, guided us through all details of the venue. There are always logistic considerations—positioning singers, conductor, soloists, orchestra, chorus and audience—but we decided that, although this would be a new venue, the beautiful church could accommodate us very well. Additionally, we adopted a plan with the maximum use of volunteers, from flowers supplied by local nurseries to moving and constructing the chorus risers ourselves.

The B Minor Mass is an important and historic piece, but not often performed because of the technical difficulties of the music. Our conductor and music director, Jo Anne Wasserman, believed the chorus had the capability to accomplish the singing and urged that we take on the challenge. Bach composed the Mass toward the end of his life, at the height of his abilities, which some believe to be that of the most formidable musician of all time. Personally, I had been introduced to the piece while at college, listening to a recording that was an inspiration to me. Even though I had wide-ranging musical preferences, and many "331/3" records on my shelf, the Mass always stood out. Now, the prospect of actually singing music that I had enjoyed hearing for over fifty-five years was a mind-blowing challenge. Kate was similarly enthusiastic but somewhat more realistic in wondering if we could accomplish the task of the performance, plus securing the necessary audience and patron support.

The Society determination was fuelled by the sheer beauty of Bach's choral music and the B Minor Mass in particular. The piece has layers and complexities that almost exceed the listener's ability to hear and understand. Other choral pieces have their beauty and brilliance, but this music contains all that, with an added abundance that totally inspires and challenges the listener. An audience might wander out of Handel's Messiah happily humming a theme, but Bach's B Minor reaches beyond that, almost overwhelming the patrons with a sense of fulfillment, possibly without their comprehending all the details.

Once the Society decided on music and venue, we next turned to the inevitable question of budget. Even though we had planned for a low-cost venue, and other more modest options than usual, there were still considerable expenses. We try to predict expenditures as accurately as possible, including every forecast of costs attributable to the event. Adding up the predicted B Minor expenses of orchestra, soloists, publicity, set-up, church, program, patron entertainment, and miscellaneous, we arrived at a budget of $63,000. Those who deal with major chorales and symphonies would call this a very low figure, but with our volunteers and in a modest venue this was a reasonable estimate.

In the current economy, raising the funds would present a challenge, and we knew we had to have the pledges and cash in hand before we committed ourselves. Fortunately, an anonymous angel made a $25,000 contribution to underwrite the project. Additionally, a $5,000 sponsorship from the Santa Barbara Bank and Trust, and a program underwriting of $2,000 from the Curtis Winery put us halfway home. We planned for thirty patrons at $250 each for a total of $7,500, and an audience estimate of nine hundred at a $25 ticket price would add $22,500. On this basis, the concert expenses were more than covered. When all was settled up after the concert, we finished almost on budget, except our audience predictions turned out to be disappointing.

To add substance to the occasion, the popular Santa Barbara resident Catholic Bishop Thomas Curry, agreed to be our guest of honor. We also offered to sing the concert in memory of individuals our patrons wished to commemorate. Both these ideas proved to be positive additions to the performance. The real challenge was to attract an audience; to help in this, all Society members solicited their friends and families to add to the limited amount of advertising we could afford and free publicity where we could find it. However, we knew we had a problem with this sophisticated piece of music, unlike either a friendly pops concert or a sentimental favorite that might include a host of children singing familiar tunes to set the audience humming.

There is a business reality to the splendor of choral singing and, for that matter, performing arts organizations everywhere: they are all in competition with one another and share the reality of fundraising and audience attendance. In the month of March alone, the Santa Barbara community had an opportunity to attend numerous events: Opera Santa Barbara's *La Traviata*; a performance of the Santa Barbara Symphony; the University of California's Chamber Choir; a Brazilian Carnival Dance Troop; the Joffrey Ballet; the Monty Python *Spamalot* stage production; Balle Foclorico Da Rio; a number of jazz concerts; community theater plays; a host of films; famous acts at the local Chumash Tribe Casino; or the option of not attending anything and just sit home and watch shows on TV. All of these productions represent their own art well, and also work hard to attract an audience.

On a regular basis, Opera Santa Barbara, the Santa Barbara Symphony, the State Street Ballet, and our Santa Barbara Choral Society are the resident companies of our fifteen-hundred seat Granada Theater. The opera seems to garner important society support, the symphony is the pride of the music community, the ballet has its aficionados, and the numerous performing music and theater groups all have their boards of directors and fund-raising programs. No artistic group functions without significant donation support; and the business realities of the performing arts community, and very much their burden of existence, are patrons and ticket purchases. In the Santa Barbara area, with a population of some 225,000, there is only so much donor support and audience available to attend a performance. Hence, competition is always a reality, and particularly in the 2012 financial times.

The good news for those of us who watch our personal budgets is that choral singing is a bargain in which to participate, compared to most retirement endeavors. There are no lost golf balls, gardening fertilizer, wasted canvases, hungry horses, or other regular expenses to worry about if one chooses music for an avocation. Choral productions are also a bargain for the community because singers volunteer their talents. Thus, for ongoing financial impact, beauty wins out over business considerations every time, with choral singing as a low budget personal occupation, as well as a bargain entertainment production.

The old saying is too true: you are what you eat. A civilization, country, or even a community, is a reflection of the activities it pursues. If a community prizes and engages in mud wrestling there will be a significant difference from a community that prizes chess matches. If the entertainment is Rave concerts, people will be different from those who pursue Beethoven. If our country fixates on sex and "Looneytoons," our future generations might wonder why superior cultures are passing us by. The indications are that while we are cutting music from our schools and starving our orchestras and chorales, other countries are pulling ahead artistically. England, while certainly no wealthier than the United States, has more singing both in churches and concerts. China has hundreds of millions studying music, and their concerts are packed. We should, indeed, be worried that the Santa Barbara County Bowl fills with an audience to hear a girl in Lady Gaga imitation spangles shouting her lungs out, a plethora of loud speakers blaring, and banks of lights flashing. Meanwhile, in the San Roque Church the home team is performing the greatest choral work in the world—and looking for an audience.

In the event, despite our efforts, the B Minor concert missed our attendance prediction, losing us the much needed ticket revenue. Of course, we ourselves had infinite satisfaction in performing the incredible music and, for most of us, the pleasure of singing a great work is more important than securing an audience.

The Bach *B Minor Mass*, in addition to being sublime, is a fiercely difficult piece to perform. Not every chorale would want to undertake the challenge, and some of our singing members chose to drop out and listen rather than face the ordeal of learning the piece. Some of the movements seem to go on forever, with combinations of challenging and ever-changing runs, and often with each chorus section singing different music lines and words simultaneously. We started rehearsing six months before the concert, and some believed that was barely enough time. Personally, I practiced every day, and confess that I made mistakes each time we rehearsed and also in both performances but, fortunately, not major or audible blunders. Before the dress rehearsal, I turned to my friend Bob Lally and said, "I think I'm making real progress and will be ready by May!" Of course the concert was in March.

Most great choral music contains a logic and pattern that help the singer along and provide clues to catch up or tone up if one goes astray. Bach, at times, seems like a runaway freight train, and the slightest lapse of attention or mistaken note will leave the singer watching a disappearing caboose running down the track. There are numerous places where breathing at the proper moment is critical and a missed breath would result in an inability to complete a phrase. Most works are more forgiving. In the fast pace of the "Cum Sancto Spiritu" there is one section where the first and second sopranos, the altos, the tenors and the basses are all singing a totally different Gloria for five measures at a very rapid pace, until, hopefully, they arrive together at the "I" of "Dei." And this is only one of many sections in my music book plaintively marked by me "watch," "study," or "caution."

The concert turned out to be one of the best performances of the Society, and very well received. One member of the audience wrote that the moving first four measures had "blown him away and captured his total attention for an inspirational and emotional concert." The audience gave us an enthusiastic standing ovation, and we had the satisfaction of knowing we had successfully accomplished a great and very difficult piece of music. To the delight of the Society Board, we completed the concert almost exactly on budget, even with a smaller than estimated audience.

We sang Saturday night and Sunday afternoon, and during the last half of the second concert, I sensed that the chorus shared the thought that most of us might never again have the opportunity to sing this amazing Bach work. We became somewhat emotional in our singing. When a hundred voices begin to be carried away in the space of a church, the results can be astounding. The strict discipline of the chorus may have suffered when this happened, but we sang full of an excitement that conveyed our feelings and dedication to the audience, adding true meaning to our performance.

The memory of this Bach B Minor will stay with us forever in our singing reminiscences, and was worth every difficulty of the business struggle, and every long moment of learning the beauty of the musical masterpiece. Kate and I felt completely fulfilled and wrung-out driving back home after the Sunday concert, but very pleased with ourselves. The Society had accomplished a major performance event, and through hard work and careful planning had also accomplished a sound economic resolution: a minor arts miracle.

Chapter Nine

CEREMONIAL DIMENSIONS

• • •

IF I HAVE LEARNED ANYTHING in my years of choral singing, it is that events and performances need timely and thorough conceptual planning to be successful. Perhaps I enjoy the Evensong service because it is brilliantly conceived to be an acceptable length, with predictable sections that can be varied and elaborate, but within an aesthetically pleasing and user-friendly framework. When a performance or religious service departs from careful, well-thought-out planning, the result can be as harmless as boredom, or as counterproductive as ill will, and possible walkout.

In May 2010, the Episcopal Diocese of Los Angeles was excited about the upcoming consecration of two new bishops to replace two who were retiring, a very important moment in the Southern California church, and historical because both incoming bishops were women. Ambitious ideas for the ceremony were discussed for months, and a combined traditional and modern service was designed to reflect the important occasion. One of the plans was for a large chorus and, accordingly, local Episcopal choirs from all over the Diocese were solicited for volunteers. On the big day, Kate and I joined some 150 singers who arrived on Saturday with their home team choir robes, assembling per instructions for rehearsal at 10:00 a.m. before the 12:30 ceremony.

The Ordination and Consecration was to take place in the Long Beach Convention Arena, capable of seating thousands, with a large stage-like altar built for the occasion in the center. Our choir bleachers were behind this raised platform, giving us a good view of the proceedings, and also of the back stage organizational drama. The Episcopal Church is at its best with familiar liturgy, and less certain with creative and expanded ceremonies, and only extensive rehearsal could have managed what turned out to be a major extravaganza. The good intentions and positive spirits of the occasion would count for much, but the enthusiastic scope of the plans needed editing and economy of scale.

As instructed, after checking in and affixing our identifying bracelets, the singers congregated in the vast backstage and, on schedule, trooped in for the rehearsal to our four rows of bleachers. The first problem became immediately obvious: most singers had only a limited view of the conductor from the ends of the long rows and there was insufficient lighting, and no time to sort out for size. Some taller singers obscured those behind, and we learned to live with the darkness. With only one hour to practice and no time for rearranging, David York, our director, told those of us in the center front to remain seated, although singers prefer to sing out from a standing position, and those at the ends to curve around for a better view of the conductor. This arrangement did not work well and got us off to a shaky start.

Singers tend to perform better when placed beside those they know and trust, and the best combination of voice placement will bring more satisfaction and accuracy in every voice. Consequently, there is a subtle and continual shuffle in most choruses as everyone tries to upgrade one's immediate neighbor, or at least sing with similarly able voices. On this occasion, I lucked out by clinging to an authoritative bass, David Pretzer, choir director of St. Gregory's, Long Beach. We saved a seat between us for Bill Eldon, who proved to have a deep and accurate voice. On the other side, I was fortunate to have Paul Elder, an Englishman, who was an accomplished bass. We settled into our third-row seats at the center, in front of the conductor, and I noticed that Kate was happily in the front row of the alto section with a friend from St. Mark's, Rinda Brown.

The large choir was allotted an hour to rehearse before other groups performing in the ceremony took over the facility for their brief rehearsals. Although we had been sent some of the intended music, and most of us had tried to learn the program, there were unfamiliar pieces given to us at rehearsal. We were assembled in a new setting, new neighbors, new conductor, limited vision, strange acoustics, and a truly daunting schedule of music. Nevertheless, despite the creative and ambitious program, we were all up for the challenge and ready to have a grand time of it.

We began with a Nigerian folksong anthem, "Jesus We Want to Meet," to be followed by a general hymn, "Lord you give the great commission..." then a sung Psalm in a beautiful arrangement new to most of us, then a chant, "Veni Sancte Spiritus." Following that was an anthem, "Christ is Made the Sure Foundation," then another hymn, "Sing a New Church," then a Sanctus, to be sung partly in Spanish, then another anthem, "The Disciples Knew the Lord Jesus." After that there was yet another anthem, "Consecration," then a hymn, "The Servant Song." Toward the end we were supposed to sing the familiar simple and lyrical hymn, "Come My

Way, My Truth, My Life," but that was dropped during the ceremony, and lastly a hymn, "This Little Light of Mine," that better belonged around a campfire. I do not know if any of us in the choir had ever faced such an extensive lineup of music on such short notice.

David York made a brave effort to rehearse his assembled singers in the anxious practice hour, with the additional challenge of bringing in various brass and percussion instruments to accompany us in the background. Most of the choir went off shaking their heads and wondering what was to come, but all were determined to do our best.

When we took our places for the ceremony, we soon discovered we were in for a siege. The first program item was a half-hour blessing, complete with smoke and feathers, from the Tongva, Chumash, Tataviam, and Acjachemem Indian tribes, indigenous to the area. This was followed by a Filipino dance group, a Chinese dance group, a flute and singing group, and then a beautiful solo rendition of "All My Trials, Lord." We now had a sense of the scope of ceremony to come, as these were only the openers. There was a distinct impression that each performing group made the most of the big stage and audience and enhanced their part in the procedures, and the unrehearsed entrances and exits took precious moments as the bustling stage producers did their best to organize the disparate groups.

The formal assembly next processed to their seats; this included families, honored guests, Diocesan staff, civic leaders, interfaith guests, clergy, visiting bishops, diocesan bishops, and finally our local bishop. The gathered clergy in their robes made a colorful and impressive display, and the ceremony proceeded with elaborate style.

While sitting in the choir bleachers during the long service, there was plenty of time to think about what we were doing, why we were doing it, and our place in the makeup of the elaborate ceremony. After years in management and politics I am quite familiar with the process of conceiving and producing ceremonies such as this, and I was very happy to have escaped the inevitable disagreements I would have had with these planners. The event clearly demonstrated the modern trend for broad relevancy and culturally inclusive participation, as opposed to traditional liturgy and ceremony. Sitting with the choir, participating as well as I knew how, and working hard to produce a pleasing musical element as directed, was a limited role that suited me perfectly. The musician situation is one of support, participation, and contribution without managerial responsibilities; and that position, much like that of a cook, a security guard, gardener, or lighting technician has much to recommend it.

Since Henry Eighth first left the Roman fold, the Episcopal church has always been a place of creative thought, and this sometimes causes it to go too far, in the opinion of some members. The progressive cultural issues of our present days have induced some conservative Episcopal parishes to leave the American church and join with a more conservative African Diocese. On the other hand, more liberal parishes have become activists for worthy, but primarily political, causes and have drifted from the Episcopal liturgy. I have been drawn into these debates but have no wish to do so anymore. That does not imply that I have diminished my own participation and responsibilities, or failed in my enthusiasm for the church. I have always loved an image from the 84th Psalm, "I had rather be a doorkeeper in the house of my God..." and in the past I have prayed to be allowed to sweep the steps in Heaven rather than seek any more preferred status. Recently, though, I now have another prayerful ambition: I long to sing in heaven.

If there are to be any disagreements or competitions alive in our church on the liturgy, ceremony, or points of theology, I fall back on that famous Western saloon sign: "Don't shoot me, I'm just the piano player."

The ceremony continued for four long hours with drums, chants, and dancing from all sectors of the Los Angeles community, much enlarging the traditional form of service. Our chorus sat, sang, and marveled as the full majesty of the day unfolded. Our own singing varied from moments of beautifully massed harmony, to agonizing moments of confusion and near choral breakdowns as we made every effort to accomplish the full schedule of music assigned. Some of the non-singing members of our local congregation in the audience reported that we sounded good and that the entire ceremony was an inspiration, but it was difficult to know that from where we sat. I can only hope that was the general opinion. From our distant positions in the choir, Kate and I exchanged glances that might be interpreted as: "All things considered, we'd rather be gardening."

The ambitious ceremony completely illustrated the time-honored phrase, "Less is more." Additionally, the inclusion of every conceivable Southern California cultural and ethnic entity seemed to indicate a lack of confidence in the heritage of the Episcopal Church. American jazz dancers would never be included in a Japanese memorial ceremony, nor would rugby players have any place in a Spanish bull ring. Kate's and my impressions were that the pride in the occasion was diminished by the overreaching ambition to make a big statement.

The important music lesson of the long afternoon was the need to consider the standard of voices, rehearsal time available, placement of singers and conductor, and then give the assembled musicians the comfort and confidence to do their best.

Chapter Ten

SONGS OF PRAISE

• • •

MUSIC, WHETHER A BASIC drumbeat chant or elaborate symphonic composition, has always been a part of religious expression. Singing is both appropriate and spiritual in worship and comes in many forms. Kate and I have been pleased to participate in a number of occasions experiencing religious music that is different from our Episcopal heritage, and here are three examples of our adventures.

Westmont College, in the oak-studded hills south of Santa Barbara, is a two-thousand-student liberal arts college with a sterling reputation. The institution has prospered since 1937 with a strong Christian religious heritage. In the 1990s the music department experienced growth and had ambitions to become a leading school in the West for music majors. To help the department, a group of outside supporters formed the Westmont Music Council as a resource and liaison with the local community. When I became a member of the council and a friend of the department, the choral director, Michael Schasberger, invited Kate and me to join the Westmont Chorus, along with a few alumni singers, in the annual Masterworks concert.

We were to sing Mozart's Requiem, a beautiful piece of music and one of the all-time classics. Kate and I dusted off our music scores and stirred our memories, as we had sung it before with the Choral Society and looked forward to the college experience. We arrived at the first rehearsal day and took our places, feeling like ancients as the young, spirited students bounced into the room. They were universally pleasant, eager, and a joy to meet. Compared to our Choral Society, there was more horseplay, energy, and a Christian evangelical atmosphere. A youthful chorus has a lighter sound, and we in the old guard stood a little straighter and tried to match the fresh voices. I rejoiced to look across and see Kate happily surrounded by young lovelies. There were perhaps seven or eight alumni and friends singing with eighty students.

After warming up, we launched into the Mozart. I was familiar with the work, but noticed that my neighbor was struggling somewhat to keep up. During a pause, I was astonished to learn that he had never seen the music before. He was a very talented music major and, a few sessions later, he practically knew the piece by heart. Mozart is serious music, and not the stuff for novices, but the young seemed to take to it naturally. Nevertheless, hearing the Mozart in the rehearsals, and then with the orchestra, reminded me that successful choral works require training, ability, and hard work.

After three months of work, we seemed to have the Requiem in hand as a chorus, but our first rehearsal with the Westmont orchestra went, as they say, medium well. When the orchestra and chorus were all assembled for that first combined session, the students spontaneously prayed, as this was a Christian-oriented college and moments of quiet reflection were a student tradition. This first altogether run-through was just after spring break, and the students were rusty. The quality of sound seemed more tentative than it should be with the concert only a few days away. On the scale from school recital quality to professional concert rank, the performance was hovering in the middle ground, and leaning toward recital. Kate and I now were also joined by our friend Bob Lally who volunteered to help in the bass section. We were still happy to be along for the ride, but hoped the students would be able to pull off a real concert.

The dress rehearsal, on the evening before the concert, was held in the large First Presbyterian Church. After some rearranging, we took our places in the choir stalls and launched into the piece, again after a short religious dedication. Everything seemed to go well, but we learned that interspersed readings would be an additional part of the performance, and there was confusion about placing the reader and soloists. As in the previous rehearsals there was some joshing and joking, and we even began to wonder if the spring season was playing with student minds. The music improved markedly in this final rehearsal, but Kate, Bob, and I wondered about the flow of the performance, and we all prayed in our own way for a smooth finale. There is a time-honored show-business belief that a bumpy rehearsal leads to a great performance. We handled the first part.

Years ago I competed in a two-day, cattle-cutting-horse competition. My horse was a quality stock horse and could look good in the cutting class, although this was not my usual competition. On the night before the first go-round, I had fallen into bad company and even worse ways, and woke up with a fierce hangover. That morning, I slapped on the saddle just in time, made it to the arena, and had a rough session and received a poor score. It hurt me to look so sloppy, so the next day I determined to campaign better as a changed man. I rose early, fed, watered, hosed down, and shined my horse, and carefully cleaned myself and the tack. Well before the event we were ready and warmed up, prepared and focused. The judge was a knowledgeable, sarcastic horseman, who was commenting on the mike continuously during the event, and as this was an all-boys event, he could say what he wanted and how he wanted to say it. The moment I walked into the arena, before I even looked at the cattle, he spotted the difference. In a sarcastic way, he drawled something close to, "Well, guess what? Brooks has got his stuff together today."

Likewise, the moment the Westmont orchestra and chorus walked into our warm-up room I could sense that their stuff was together. Of course, they all looked the part, turned out in black formal dresses and tuxedos, but more than that, they seemed ready and focused. We sat quietly, and after going through warm-up voice exercises, Director Michael Shasberger gave what I can only describe as a locker room pep talk. Memory fades, but it went something like this: "Family, friends, and faculty are in the audience and they deserve the best we can give. We have been training and learning and we are well prepared to present a beautiful performance. The *Requiem* is one of the greatest pieces of music in the world and during its composition Mozart died, leaving this as his legacy. We are here to make it live!" His words harmonized with the focused mood, and I could sense a settling and determination. After a student offered a short, earnest prayer, everyone lined up, intent on their part and ready to sing.

We gave a performance that, by far, exceeded any of our rehearsals. All the preparation came together, and we sang a concert to make Westmont proud. The orchestra and chorus stayed together without mistakes, and the soloists gave the difficult music sincere and well-presented efforts. The words and Scripture read by the Celebrant, interspersed with the music, had worried Kate and me when he read in rehearsal, but in the performance the readings brought a focus and meaning to the music. A beaming smile on the director's face during a standing ovation from the audience told us that we had done well, and people were moved.

Our experience in that concert taught us about the next generation and their determination to represent their school and themselves with pride. The young students had purpose and inspiration, and they delivered in a way that reminded me of the expression, "the college try." Choral singing, like many things, is a reflection of the collective will, and when focused, motivated, and spiritual, singers can accomplish a great communal outcome.

* * *

Traditional Gospel music is alive and well in the lively and friendly Los Angeles West Angeles Church of God in Christ. On a Sunday in May, the congregation of over fifteen hundred and clergy headed by Bishop Charles Blake were ready for an important and lively Sunday service. The congregation was in their Sunday best and took their cathedral seats in anticipation. Above all, the music was to be powerful.

The church in the heart of Los Angeles boasts nineteen-thousand members, mostly of African American heritage, and is a true community center with many worship services as well as counseling, community development, support groups, events, and centers of activity for all ages and needs. The sanctuary holds over two thousand with large television screens and equipment to broadcast the services on radio and television. This is a well-organized and important church, and a beacon of leadership for the community.

The service began as the eighty-member choir, dressed in red and gold robes, took their places informally. They were accompanied by two piano keyboards, two electric guitars, and drums, all with professional amplification. As the ministers processed in, the keyboards began with quiet background music, then worked into a melody which the choir took up and gradually moved into a song of praise with increasing volume and excitement.

The choir music was exuberant and energetic as the singers swayed back and forth, often clapping or holding their arms in the air. Occasionally the music would subside into a background sound or lyric melody. In many of the pieces, some of the choir members would come forward to microphones and sing solos, or repeat the music phrases with enlargement and increased emphasis. The words were put up on a large screen so the congregation could join in as they wished. The small, amplified band held the driving beat, which added to the excitement and impact of the music. Once or twice the choir erupted in full-out volume and the impact was thrilling, but even the "normal" volume was formidable.

There was prayer, Scripture reading, "praise and worship," a long, lively, sermon, and communion served to the many attendees by the ushers. A prayer was offered to individuals in the congregation who were then invited to approach the altar and be escorted into a side chapel for special counseling.

This large and active church was quite different from our little country parish. The service was also infused with energy, enthusiasm, and scale beyond the traditional Episcopal liturgy. Our Evensong would have been lost in the large Cathedral just as the energetic choir volume would have startled St. Mark's congregation. The experience brought out the fact that individual Christians have much in common in prayer and love of God, but great variation in modes of expression and music.

Kate and I were able to join the Westmont and Mormon

Choirs easily with their classic music and traditional presentation, but would be very intimidated about standing with the West Angeles Church choir. Here, the musical expression was more akin to free-form jazz than Mozart, with a strong element of movement, and free expression within strict conventions. The spirit and exhilaration of the West Angeles Church choir reached out and moved the congregation, and moved me strongly. I left the church service with a craving to find a choir with the same energy and expression and learn to join in.

* * *

Perhaps the most famous American singing service is the "Music and the Spoken Word" worship and broadcast from the Mormon Tabernacle in Salt Lake City every Sunday morning. One vivid childhood memory I still cherish is my mother, ill with debilitating cancer, listening to the Tabernacle on her bedside radio. How could I ever, as a young boy, imagine that I might someday sing with that amazing choir, now in their eighty-second year of broadcasting, the longest continuing program in the country, beginning in 1929?

Fortunately, the Tabernacle Choir has a limited outreach program, and under special circumstances will invite singers to join them for the Thursday rehearsal of that week's performance, as a learning experience for those lucky enough to attend. With the help of a good friend who knew one of the singers, and after much correspondence and an application, which included our singing history and personal background, Kate and I were invited to rehearse with them.

The Church of Jesus Christ of the Latter Day Saints, popularly known as the Mormon Church, maintains their headquarters in Salt Lake City on a thirty-four-acre campus that contains the famous Mormon Temple, headquarters buildings, and the Mormon Tabernacle, known as "MO Tab," home of the choir and broadcasts. The Temple Choir of around three hundred and fifty, accompanied by a hundred and twenty members of the symphony orchestra, are all volunteers from the Mormon Church and work hard to maintain their excellent quality and reputation.

The choir's six-to-nine-month audition process is incredibly arduous, beginning with an application requiring a recommendation from their home church and local bishop. The next step is a three-hour examination, written and sung, with all the usual requirements, only more so, with a very high standard. After passing these two stages, another audition is required at which at least two pieces will be sung solo, as well as difficult tests on music theory and singing exercises. The last stage is a six-to-nine month "Choir School" probation while actually singing with a choir. A typical season might start with three hundred applicants and yield thirty singers. Those chosen are considered "set apart," in that they are carrying out their offering to God in a mission commitment by their singing.

I wondered how they were able to find three hundred brave and accomplished singers willing to undergo the audition process, and learned that the Mormon Church has a strong singing tradition for everyone in their churches, and many members who study music from an early age hoping to join the Tabernacle Choir. An informal choir was established four years after the great trek that first brought settlers to the Salt Lake area in the 1840s. Construction began on the Tabernacle building in 1857, a few years after the settlers became established. With a population of singers and a splendid building, the extraordinary institution of the Mormon Tabernacle Choir grew into its present prominence in church music. In all my experience, I have never seen as large and accomplished group of singers able to respond immediately to the director and sing exactly on the beat in unison, in harmony, and on pitch. A visit to Salt Lake City is well worth the effort, just to hear the choir.

Kate and I arrived at the appointed time at the designated entrance, after a shopping trip because Kate had not brought the appropriate dress to join with the singers. The ushers greeted us by name and sat us down in a front row while the orchestra completed their pre-rehearsal run-through. When the choir assembled, we were ushered into front row choir seats and greeted by our neighbors who were prepared for us to join in. When he heard my background, the bass next to me remarked that his father had probably sung while my mother was listening. After some announcements, there were prayers given by two church leaders, and the conductor, Mack Wilberg, launched the choir into rehearsal.

The two-and-a-half hour session, without break, was crisp and focused. Most of the music had been performed before by the singers, and they launched into each piece sounding well prepared. Each singer had a folder with music neatly arranged and containing red pencils to mark the music sheets, but only as instructed by the director, with no personal notations. The rehearsal was very focused with no chatter and complete attention from the singers. Kate and I were welcome to join in, but did so only when we were sure of the music, and then only softly.

Mack Wilberg wore a microphone that allowed him to speak over the orchestra and choir as they were playing and singing. Sometimes he altered or commented on the tempo or volume, or made specific instructions to the sections. He rarely had to repeat his comments. He called the singers "Brothers" and "Sisters" and a gentle admonishment produced instant results. He might say to the basses, "Brothers, we need a little less volume in this section." And the result could be heard immediately. The three hundred attentive singers could be steered with the slightest touch. I watched

Kate, opposite in the soprano section, and could see that she was impressed and cautiously joining in.

After running through a piece once or twice, and sorting out any problems, Director Wilberg would announce, "We're taping now!" which meant that the next run-through would be recorded to assess timing and any possible refinements that needed to be dealt with in the early morning rehearsal before broadcast.

The long Thursday night rehearsal went by too quickly for us; we enjoyed every minute. At the conclusion, Mack Wilberg asked Kate and me to stand and gave us a long introduction and welcome. The choir responded with applause that made us feel warm and accepted. I wanted to applaud *them*.

Kate and I rose early on Sunday to drive from Park City to Salt Lake for the broadcast. The clear Sunday morning drive through the Utah mountains enhanced our excitement to hear what we had experienced on Thursday and had also heard a number of times on the radio. The doors closed around 9:30 for the 10:00 broadcast, but we arrived at 8:30 to be sure of a front seat. We found the choir and orchestra in full rehearsal doing a complete run-through. On finishing, Director Wilberg announced that there were twenty-seven seconds overtime and everyone should be prepared for shorter breaks between the announcer and music and also a slightly faster tempo to some of the music. The stage, choir, and orchestra areas were crawling with camera operators, producers with clipboards, others with earphones and mikes, and a general atmosphere of countdown hustle.

The traditional half hour of broadcast was tightly timed to fit in six short pieces, interspersed with introductions and inspirational words from an announcer off stage, and ending with a sung closing blessing. There were no commercials. Today's program was: "On Great Lone Hills," by Sibelius; "Be Thou My Vision," a traditional Irish hymn; "Meditation on an Old Covenantor's Tune," by Robert Elmore; "Dear to Heart of the Shepherd," arranged by Mack Wilberg; "Who Will Buy?" from the Broadway show *Oliver*; and "Benediction" by David Warner; and lastly, the sung blessing. The broadcast ended exactly on time and without the slightest ripple or mistake. The quality of the orchestra and choir was memorable. One could understand why "Music and the Spoken Word" is the longest lasting broadcast in the country.

As we left I waved to my rehearsal bass seatmate and received a smile back as he was leaving the choir area. Kate and I emerged to find two young women missionaries who gave us a tour of the conference center. They were appropriately from Wisconsin and Oxford, England, and clearly devoted to their missionary calling. The great conference center seats twenty-one thousand and is the site for some of the choir concerts. We drove to the airport feeling that we had experienced a warm welcome and the experience of singing with one of the great choirs in the world.

Songs of praise find many different expressions around the world but, clearly, music is a universal and integral expression of worship. Kate and I hope to continue many experiences and expressions of the world's religion and singing.

Chapter Eleven

Church For All

• • •

HOMES, COMMUNITIES, TOWNS, cities, and nations are known for and by the symbols that represent the place, and when one thinks about a location, these come readily to mind. Tombstone, Arizona, has the OK Corral where everybody shot one another, and Rome has St. Peter's Basilica where the Pope waves from a balcony. Orlando has Disneyland, and Hartford has Yale. Every place has its markers and, hopefully, all of us live with symbols that will make us proud.

Washington D.C. is known for many national symbols, although the White House and Congress in their present condition of political siege may be currently out of fashion. The Washington Monument, the Smithsonian, and the Lincoln Memorial will endure, as will other Washington icons. But the most memorable symbol for many is the National Cathedral, the splendid setting for meaningful ceremonies, and sometimes for very stressful historic moments, such as the 9/11 national mourning of the destruction of the Twin Towers.

The Cathedral Church of St. Peter and St. Paul is actually Episcopal, but the mission and role of the institution is not to promote this denominational foundation, but rather to serve and be known as the country's National Cathedral. The great building strives to be a religious home for people of all faiths or no faith, to be enjoyed in contemplation of God's presence, each person in their own way. This is not an easy task for the considerable National Cathedral organization, but they work hard to do their best and are continually examining ways for worship, relevance, and participation in the many challenges of the modern world and local community.

As published, the Mission Statement of the Nation Cathedral is: "A Church for national purposes and perspectives. A unique blend of spiritual and the civic, this Episcopal Cathedral is a voice for generous-spirited Christianity and a catalyst for reconciliation and interfaith dialogue to promote respect and understanding. We invite all people to share in our commitment to create a more hopeful and just world." Many Episcopalians are uncomfortable with this modern, all-inclusive outreach to the world, but the greater purpose of the Cathedral is laudable and important to the country. It is probable that Jesus would approve of the philosophy of the institution, and might even choose the National Cathedral for a place to preach, rather than a more sectarian or insular church.

The ecumenical outreach of the National Cathedral illuminates an historical conundrum in our modern American history. How extensively do we include every religion in the world in our conversations and events to the diminution of our own historic Judeo-Christian heritage? President George Bush received a Koran from a Muslim cleric during the memorial service for the tragedy of the 9/11 World Trade Center disaster. The courts increasingly insist that we eliminate all Christian discourse and symbolism from our public institutions, while simultaneously seeming to allow and protect the practice of all other religious beliefs. Those of a philosophical mind may well wonder to what extent a nation can be all things to all people without becoming as meaningless as the Tower of Babel.

In attending our granddaughter's graduation from Amherst College, we sat through a Baccalaureate "Celebration" that included blessings by a Buddhist, Muslim, and Hindu; readings from Islamic, Hindu, Jewish, and secular poetry texts; and the Baccalaureate addressed by a Muslim Imam who gave us a lecture on tolerance. Amherst currently enjoys a substantial reputation as one of the best colleges in the nation. It has evolved from a Christian institution, although non-sectarian founded, according to one history of the college, for the classical education of indigent young men of piety and talents for the Christian ministry. However, this tradition has taken a profound turn towards secularism, symbolized by the destruction of the college church in 1949. One wonders whether current Amherst is at sea without a compass, drifting in the world's religions, philosophies, and politics.

Interestingly, Amherst is also known as "the singing college" with many groups, including the Concert Choir, Madrigal Singers, Women's Chorus, Glee Club, Zumbyes, Bluestockings, Route 9, Sabrinas, and Terras Irradient, a co-ed Christian a cappella group. There are no Amherst college chapel services or chapel choir. Any family valuing church attendance should not expect any reinforcement whatsoever from most modern campuses. Our early colleges were inspired by religious intellectual fervor, but they are now sailing in secular waters.

However, here at the Washington Cathedral, the Anglican

Episcopal embracing tradition is at its best and serves an all-inclusive, mediating force in the world, while holding steadfast to the basic articles of faith. Visitors should take pride in the extensive intellectual exploration, as well as local and world community outreach in the many activities of the National Cathedral.

Best of all, the Episcopal choral tradition provides the substance of a phenomenal music program as the Cathedral carries out its mission. Songs and choral works that have been performed in churches for centuries have been found to enhance modern purposes of relevancy and outreach. In the National Cathedral search for meaningful religious expression, traditional choral music has very much survived the contemporary tests.

The Girl and Boy Choristers, combined with a professional Men's Choir, serve as the principal Cathedral choir. Additionally, the Cathedral Choral Society, and the Cathedral Volunteer Choir, as well as an extensive program welcoming visiting choirs and choral groups to perform, continually fill the National Cathedral with splendid music. And, most important to the theme of this book, the Cathedral holds daily Evensong services. It is very gratifying that Evensong holds its place amidst cutting edge theological and ecumenical thought.

Over the altar area the pipes of the aptly named "Great Organ" are displayed, a famous instrument worthy of concerts on its own. This powerful installation of 189 ranks and 10,647 pipes appears to be driven by the wind energy of locomotive steam engines. Its heroic sound has the potential to overcome choir, congregation, and symphony orchestra if the organist gives way to the temptation of letting out the stops and loosing its tonal might. It is a musical device of great beauty and great physical power.

This immense Cathedral has clean lines, as cathedrals go, designed on classic neo-gothic architecture, and is one of the largest churches in the world. The building was begun in 1907 and mostly completed in the seventies, although detail work continues, with a setback in 2011 when an earthquake damaged the building and required extensive repairs. A visit to the building is also rewarding to see more than two hundred glass windows and numerous works of art, including the gargoyles, and even one Darth Vader drain spout decorating a high cornice.

The Girl Choristers attend the National Cathedral School and the Boy Choristers attend St. Alban's School, both campuses adjoining the Cathedral grounds. Kids with musical potential apply and audition for an opportunity to work hard in the two schools which, in turn, nurture and train the young voices as well as their minds. In exchange for substantial financial help with their schooling, the girls and boys participate regularly in singing services, produce recordings, and tour the world with the Cathedral Choir. In singing daily Evensong Services, the boys alternate with the girls, and once a week each sing with the professional men who complete the choir.

On a Thursday Evensong in October when we visited, about twenty boys and eighteen men, half on each side of the altar, made up the choir. There was a congregation of three to four hundred, and tourists in the background, quietly wandering the building. The young boys were quite professional, and sang the service with beautifully trained voices soaring to the distant ceiling. The presiding priest spoke the familiar words and the congregation spoke and sang their part into the huge Cathedral spaces. The boys—and I am sure the girls would be as well—were focused, with amazing clarity and precision. The purposeful demeanor of the choir and their musical talents demonstrated that the Cathedral experience is providing these young people the stuff of a great personal future.

Beyond these choirs and combinations of choirs, the Cathedral Choral Society can present a concert of around one-hundred-fifty trained amateurs who have passed the audition and twenty-four professional singers to lead the sections. These glorious voices, usually accompanied by a symphony orchestra, fill the vast Cathedral space with amazing sound. On a concert day in October 2010, the Cathedral Choral Society, with the Washington Symphony Orchestra, sang selections of French music with the added panache, as they do in Washington, of performing "Under the honorary patronage of His Excellency the Ambassador of France." A two-by-two entrance procession of the choir went on forever as they sang the first selection walking down the center aisle through an almost full house. Their quality of voices, and the splendid acoustics in the National Cathedral, did our Washington symbol proud.

Six years ago a new strata of National Cathedral music was formed from amateur volunteer singers to provide choral music for the early, 8:45 a.m., Sunday morning service. This unique group rises early Sunday mornings to assemble with coffee cups for a 7:30 rehearsal in the basement choir room in the depths of the Cathedral. The friendliness, dedication, and competence of the thirty-plus choir were clearly evident when I was able to visit them on a Sunday in May 2011. There had been a Thursday rehearsal also, so the group was prepared for the three choral pieces of the service. The conductor, a pleasant Englishman, Jeremy Filsell, greeted the singers and, by way of warm-up, launched them into the three congregational hymns to be sung that morning with the assistant organist accompanying on a piano.

The anthems began with "Ave Verum Corpus" by Nicholas White, which went well after some adjustments and tune-ups, then a difficult contemporary arrangement by Michael McCarthy of the "Jubilate Deo" that required a good deal of work, as the wall clock ran on unmercifully. All the singers were competent and responsive, making steady progress on each run-through and without obvious errors. It was impressive to realize that this excellent choir was only the "third string" of the Cathedral singing lineup.

The last piece was the familiar and well executed, "If Ye Love Me," by Thomas Tallis. All too soon, it was wheels up as the choir vanished to take their places in the rear of the Cathedral. In the summer, their uniform was dark pants, white shirts, and no robes.

There was a surprising turn of events at this rehearsal. The choir secretary had set me up with music sheets and a place to stand in the bass section to observe the operation. The choir stood at risers to hold the music, and my neighbor was a pleasant, competent bass, Philip Kopper, who knew what he was doing. We exchanged pleasantries and a few comments during the rehearsal. I told him about my book, *Evensong*, in progress, and he replied, "Well, that is a coincidence, because I am a publisher."

I took my seat toward the front of the congregation of three or four hundred for the 8:30 Communion Service. The choir opened with the Tallis piece, sung a cappella from the rear, as a meditation to set the mood. Their voices blended beautifully, filling the great nave, and sending shivers up one's spine and some welling behind the eyes. I contemplated on what a meaningful experience it is for a small group of people to combine their voices and transmit a warm, melodious harmony, imparting beauty and emotion. Here are some thirty singers joined to produce a fleeting moment of sound, admitted into the senses of the congregation, and inspiring aesthetic and physical, as well as spiritual, responses. How splendid the grace of choral singing!

The choir processed and took their places on risers behind the altar while the congregation struggled somewhat with the first hymn. The acoustics for the thirty-two singers in the central space of the great building, near the altar, were not as friendly as at the rear of the Cathedral, and their mid service anthem was bullied by the power of the great organ, but the overall effect provided beauty and substance. The Eucharist was enhanced and became an important service through the accompaniment of these early rising singers. There are probably not many choirs so dedicated to sing only once and early, and our National Cathedral is well served by these volunteers.

Anyone visiting Washington should see this great Cathedral on St. Alban's hill, and by all means try to hear a concert, service, or Evensong. The National Cathedral appears on national television with many special moments of rejoicing, national mourning, and other days of historic importance. And as this great church is the setting for so many future events, the building should be included on any Washington tour. Our country can be justifiably proud of this symbol. But there is one national event that our country ruled out in 1776 and will never be celebrated in the National Cathedral: a royal wedding.

Chapter Twelve

CANADA AND CREATION

● ● ●

THE BERKSHIRE CHORAL FESTIVAL is a well-managed organization that annually produces five major choral performances, three at their headquarters at a boy's boarding school in the Berkshire Mountains, Massachusetts, and two planned somewhere else around the world. The festival organization is maintained by a healthy 1982 financial grant from benefactor John Stookey, and is an inspiration and source of great pleasure to American choral singers. Our first experience with them was in Montreal in 2010. In 2011, they went to Vancouver and Salzburg, which we attended and is described later in the book. In the fall of 2012, they will go to Edinburgh, and we plan to join them there.

The chorus for each performance is drawn from qualified amateur American singers who subscribe to the cost of attending a session. The singers must be experienced, and either known to the festival staff, auditioned, or have submitted credentials to participate. They are sent the music score and a learning CD well in advance, and are expected to know the planned performance before arriving to experience an intense week of rehearsals prior to the concert. The orchestra is always a first-class local organization, and the conductors recruited for the event are outstanding international choral figures. The Festival serves as excellent American goodwill ambassadors wherever they go in the world.

The works performed are famous and challenging choral compositions, and the venues, outside the Berkshire campus, are impressive and usually attended by large and enthusiastic local audiences. The Berkshire school includes a magnificent indoor sports facility that doubles as a concert hall and easily accommodates chorus, orchestra, and audience. Serious choral singers in the United States, sooner or later, come to know of, and many participate in, the festival events.

In 2010, Kate and I applied for a week in Montreal to sing Joseph Haydn's oratorio, *The Creation*, a splendid and challenging Austrian classic, under the direction of the famous English conductor, Jane Glover. *The Creation* was written in the 1790s, a period of history when a young America was beginning to understand the governance of a new country independent from England. *The Creation* is a musical rendition of the book of Genesis, the biblical story of the creation of the world. The first performance in Vienna, in 1798, was attended by a select, important group of invitees with a huge crowd outside the small theater trying to catch whatever parts of the new masterpiece they could hear. It has played to audiences successfully ever since.

This would be a new adventure for us and we were very pleased when we were accepted to join the chorus. On the application, Berkshire asked for the works that I had sung during the last three years. With the full schedule of the Santa Barbara Choral Society, my list was impressive. Of course, I had only been with them three years. Before that, my record was blank, but, luckily, Berkshire did not ask about that. Most of the chorus had sung for many years.

As a bonus, Kate's talented sister, Sarah DeLima, agreed to drive up from Boston and join us for the week. She is a professional actor who has sung in musicals and has a wicked sense of humor. I was afraid she might start taking off on the German pronunciation of the Haydn work and interfere with my concentration, but the music was one of her favorite pieces, one that she had always wanted to sing, so she was all enthusiasm and concentration.

My personal preparation to learn *The Creation* began in December, prior to the July concert. I read the score, studied the German, picked out the notes on the piano, sang with the learning CD, sang with my teachers Rose Knoles and Ken Ryals, and even began to sing the music in my dreams. I was determined to know the piece when I arrived in Montreal. The learning curve is embarrassingly long for me, but I actually enjoyed every minute of the hours of study and practice. When you love doing something, it is not a chore, and the music learning preparation is, for me, much of the fun.

We arrived at the Montreal McGill University residence hotel two days early to adapt to the time change and enjoy the famous city, which included, we discovered, the annual jazz festival. We toured the sights, took in the St. Lawrence River trip and reveled in Canadian energy and friendliness. Saturday afternoon enabled us to attend the Anglican Christ Church Cathedral, where a small but excellent choir performed an Evensong in the proper tradition, even though the lessons and liturgy were in French. The congregation was not large, but the service was broadcast on the radio, giving us visions of distant trappers in their lonely cabins in the French Canadian wilderness joining in with the prayers. We walked Montreal like tourists; but Kate and I, with the prospect of performing for the city, also felt a part of the community.

When Monday morning rehearsal began on the first day of preparation for the concert to be performed in one week, we took our seats somewhat apprehensively in the alto and bass sections. Many of the attendees sat with friends from former concerts, and some claimed the front rows; but for me as a newcomer, it was sitting by chance. Kate and Sarah, worried about seeing the conductor, firmly decided to position themselves in the front row throughout the week, so they might see and hear Jane Glover easily.

The qualities of an effective conductor are similar to the varied but compelling charismatic attributes of all effective leaders. The music director mounts the podium and must capture the attention of the chorus with a variety of characteristics that can vary from passive and friendly, to aggressive and assertive. This leader must command respect and willingness from the singers who will follow and respond sensitively to the director's every nuanced movement. Generals Eisenhower, Montgomery, Patton, Rommel, and Bradley all had very different mannerisms and reputations, but they all led and won battles with their unique styles, and so do choral directors.

Of course the director must know the composition and all aspects of music theory, in addition to vocal tone and qualities. But somehow the leadership of a chorus is more immediately personal than the leadership of an orchestra. It is interesting that certain conductors are known for their instrumental leadership quite differently from their choral leadership, because there is more technical necessity in the former and more nurturing necessary in the latter. Choral conductors deal with the minds and emotions of the singers in more involved and compelling personal relationships than do instrumental conductors.

Jane Glover turned out to be charming, witty, demanding,

and persuasive—in the most insisting manner. She was able to affably round up this stray herd of one-hundred-and-forty singers and move them in the direction she desired. Even on the first day she somehow got us to produce the sound of a trained chorus accustomed to singing together. She stood on the podium before us, conjuring with her smile; critical, supportive, and inspirational with her pencil held as a baton. We all felt the steel will behind the friendly and engaging personality.

"Der Herr ist Gross, in seiner macht, und ewig bleight sein ruhm!" (The Lord is great, and great his might, his glory lasts evermore), Franz Joseph Haydn, *Die Schopfung* (The Creation), was very much in German and, for us Yankees, pronunciation was an added hurdle to the classic piece of music.

Rehearsals ran two hours, twice a day, with concentrated work on the famous Haydn sections. Little by little this random group of dedicated singers, who aspired to reproduce the historical work, began to come together. We toiled daily and unendingly on our German pronunciation with Jane Glover insisting on clear diction. The choral diplomacy of accepting one another's pitch and rhythm with equanimity prevailed in the bass section, although Kate later informed me that glances and murmurs of concern about singers were more openly displayed among the altos. There were clearly stronger and weaker voices, and the experienced hands maneuvered to sit next to the best, and away from the problem singers. As far as I could tell, there were no obvious complaints or heads turning as mistakes were made in my bass section.

Choral singing is a team sport and a dominant neighbor can either lead a section astray or provide an influence toward a stellar performance. Fortunately, the better voices began to prevail in the chorus. During the week I had good, and less good, company as the seating shifted, but never a real neighborhood problem. Even the best singers are concerned about the possibility of making an obvious mistake by coming in at the wrong moment or otherwise departing from the herd. Most singers are also haunted by never quite knowing the quality of their own voice. I craved to know my various neighbors' feelings about my sound, but I would never ask in this polite and friendly company. Kate and I, and doubtless everyone else, would unburden ourselves gossiping about a neighbor's performance in private conversations together. These opinions and feelings could run strong about various voices and personalities, but we never gave away anything in session.

As the group came to know one another and make new friends, we toured the city, dined at the cafes, and exchanged adventures. A new friend in the bass section dragged the three of us to an Ethiopian restaurant, doubtless enjoying the date with sister Sarah. Kate and I were skeptical, but can now happily recommend Ethiopian dining, even in Montreal. Cold, refreshing, Moosehead beer became a lifesaver in the heat wave as we came to know our new chorus in the outdoor cafes.

The demanding work of long rehearsals, and the quest for a great performance, united us in a common effort. The dreaded moment would come to almost all of us when Jane Glover singled out a section, or part of a section, to admonish, inspire, and bring us to the correct pitch, timing, pronunciation, or attention to her direction. Sometimes we sat like guilty schoolchildren, knowing we could do better and wanting to please the conductor. The bass section took satisfaction when the sopranos were worked over, but we always knew it could be our turn next. Fortunately, a pub down the road provided late night unwinding, sustenance, and Moosehead on tap to relieve the rehearsal tension. Finally, we moved from the hotel ballroom to the Eglise St. Jean Baptiste and mounted the risers to rehearse with the McGill Concert Orchestra. A record heat wave caused us concern about our performance and audience turnout, and even in the huge church the hot weather debilitated our efforts as we perspired and labored through rehearsal.

The concert day proved somewhat cooler, complete with intermittent rain that did not discourage the large audience that filled the church. *The Creation* is a big piece of music, telling a big story. The orchestra soared when needed, and the professional soloists, brought in for the occasion from New York operas, were outstanding. Our chorus gave their all with a very acceptable rendition of the difficult passages, without obvious errors, and with a full quality, glorious choral sound. Here we were—new acquaintances from all over the country, united in voices as only a large chorus can experience. Personally, I felt I was keeping up with my neighbors and was a small but very real contributor to the beauty of the piece.

The music begins with an overture deliberately written with catchy rhythms and slight atonal notes that appear to be mistakes, depicting the chaos before creation. The chorus then enters, as quietly and intensely as one-hundred-and-fifty voices can manage, while holding the pitch in a sotto voice undertone, singing:

"Und der Geist Gottes schwebe auf der flache der wasser; und Gott sprach; es wer de licht; und es ward Licht!" Or, "And the Spirit of God moved upon the face of the waters; and God said; let there be light; and there was Light."

On the word "light" we moved suddenly to a held, strong, majestic forte, and our chorus reveled in the moment. The oratorio continues with descriptive words and tones telling the story in all its drama and emotions. The last chorus was a glorious conclusion: *"Singst dem Herren alle stimmen!"* Or, "Sing the Lord ye voices all!" And, *"Des Herren ruhm, er bleibt in ewigkeit!"* Or, "The Lord is great, his praise shall last forever!"

The performance came off without a mistake and with an emotion that reflected the substance of the story. The audience gave us a standing ovation.

Sarah drove us to the airport early next morning in an afterglow of satisfaction and sadness at the end of the experience. How incredible to visit a new city, meet new friends, and engage in a demanding and rewarding musical adventure. We had accomplished a career milestone; we performed new music with an unknown conductor and unknown singers and were proud of our work. We had heard that Berkshire planned to travel to Salzburg the next year and looked forward to the possibility of working that trip into our singing career.

Brooks and Kate with her father, the Very Reverend Walter Boulton, in 1958 at the Guildford Cathedral where they were destined to sing Evensong fifty three years later.

Kate, dressed as a skater, poses for a Royal Ballet publicity photo.

In 2011, Brooks and Kate are singing Evensong sitting in the cantoris side of the Guildford Cathedral choir stalls, opposite the singers on the decanis side.

Kate is dancing during a Royal Ballet rehearsal.

Kate escorted by her brother John arrives for her wedding in 1958 on the Guildford High Street.

Brooks and Kate
harvesting grapes
in 1975.

Brooks and Kate are gathering cattle in the early 1980s on the
San Antonio Ranch.

Brooks inducts Kate into the Societe Mondiale du Vin of the Chaine des Rotisseurs.

The Saint Mark's choir, in rehearsal, led by Rose Knoles. Brooks is second from the right, Kate is on the aisle in the second row.

Kate, front and center, sings a rehearsal with the Santa Barbara Choral Society. Brooks is above left, almost out of the frame .

Brooks sings with the basses in the Santa Barbara Choral Society rehearsal.

Brooks, top right, sings a formal concert with the Santa Barbara
Choral Society.

The Santa Barbara Choral Society, singing in full concert, at the
Granada Theater.

Kate is presented to the Queen of England and uses her ballet form to good advantage.

Kate, second row third from right, and Brooks, fourth from left in back row, sing a concert with the Westmont College Chorus.

Brooks, front row, second from the right, and Kate, front row, second from the left, rehearsing with the Mormon Tabernacle Choir and Orchestra.

Life does not get any better than singing with three grand-daughters. From left: Molly, Samantha and Fiona.

We are rehearsing the Verdi *Requiem* in the London Royal Albert Hall with Bart's Choir. Kate is with the sopranos in the upper left and Brooks is with the basses in the front row. There are four hundred singers with the Royal Philharmonic Orchestra.

Santa Barbara Choral Society touring group singing in the Barcelona Cathedral, June 2011. Brooks, Kate, daughter Hayley and granddaughters Georgina and Fiona are in the chorus.

" *Berkshire Choral Festival* "   Salzburg - Mondsee 2011

Singing with the Berkshire Choral Festival on the steps where Julie Andrews and Chrisopher Plummer were married in the *Sound of Music*. Kate is with the Sopranos, fifth row second from left, and Brooks is in the top row, fourth from left.

Chapter Thirteen

CHRISTMAS JOY

● ● ●

IN 1741 GEORGE FREDERICK HANDEL composed the *Messiah*, and it has become one of the best known and most frequently performed choral works in history. Speaking as a singer, I find this work an amazing and uplifting experience; even those who are not necessarily regular members of a chorus seem to enjoy having a go at joining their voices in the great work. Concerts where the *Messiah* chorus parts are open to all volunteers—the *Messiah* sing-a-longs—have become a fixture in the Christmas season.

For more than thirty years a December *Messiah* sing-a-long has been held in the Santa Barbara first Presbyterian Church, with participation in the choir open to everyone who makes a ten-dollar contribution. This event is looked forward to by many locals during the Christmas season.

There are few formalities, and the sing-a-long concert has the virtue of simplicity. All singing participants pay ten dollars and all orchestra musicians and miscellaneous staff are volunteers. There are no expenses and all the proceeds for the last few years have been given to the Food Bank, adding to the satisfaction of participating in the performance. There are many locals who cannot begin the Christmas season before this *Messiah* event and, although they might sing nothing else throughout the year, happily dust off their music scores on the second Tuesday in December to do their best.

The event, an inspiration of classic music radio station owner Bob Scott, is managed by our local Santa Barbara Foundation, the source of support for many worthy causes. Radio station sponsorship adds a great benefit to the concert because KDB 97.3 FM rebroadcasts the concert so that everyone can hear themselves sing at a later date. On a typical performance, as many as four-hundred chorus members will attend. This is truly the stuff that makes a community worthwhile.

A well-known jazz pianist, Jim Pugh, when he is not touring, sometimes sings with our St. Mark's choir. We usually stand next to each other and he is a pleasure to have in the bass section. Although he knows the relatively simple anthem scores inside out technically, he is not usually a singer, and enjoys the challenge of our bass music as a relief from road gigs. A couple of years ago Jim and I decided to drive down to the *Messiah* sing-a-long to see what all the excitement was about. We arrived in time for the short rehearsal, paid ten dollars, and took our places in the phalanx of well over a hundred basses. I recognized a few Choral Society members, but most of the friendly and upbeat assembled company were strangers. We all greeted one another warmly, with common purpose, pleasure, and enthusiasm for the experience, but probably all wondering about one another's talents.

The volunteer orchestra sat in the chancel, the conductor stood on a podium in front, the soloists were in the front pew, and the crowd of singers sat as a congregation in the large church, grouped under "Soprano," "Alto," "Tenor," and "Bass" signs. The conductor gave us a brief pep talk, suggesting we try to stay with his beat as well as with the notes, words, and other notations in the score, then launched our rehearsal. As one might expect, there were some creative interpretations, but generally, the sound was impressive. Jim and I felt happy with our neighbors; although in that type of volunteer group there were the usual missed notes and original timing. There are always leaders who will sing out and followers who will join, and our robust company made adjustments to their neighbors and settled. The rehearsal lasted about forty-five minutes and established the entrances to the parts of the work we were performing.

As the concert time approached, an audience filtered in, contributed to the Food Bank, and took seats behind the chorus and in the balcony of the large church. A few slid in beside friends and relations in the chorus, adding to the friendly and informal atmosphere of the occasion. We all applauded the conductor as he took the podium. He tentatively smiled at us and we were away.

The parts of the lengthy piece we were to sing were familiar and seemingly straightforward, but there are always tricky sections and pitfalls in a great work. The quality of music was amazingly good for the crowd of amateurs, although there were some worrisome moments where groups of individuals forged ahead or lagged behind the beat. The pace and words move along rapidly, and I noticed a number of our neighbors drifting out of contention and then lustily rejoining on the familiar parts. Additionally, some singers were more familiar with *Messiah* recordings than music scores, and strayed into the melody line rather than stay with the more prosaic harmonies written for their parts on the music score. The exalted melody line is usually the province of the sopranos.

Another aspect of choral singing crept into the bass section during the more approachable parts of the work. Sometimes individual singers in a group become slightly competitive and try to outdo one another, although usually in a positive manner. I won't say that on this occasion there was rivalry or aggression, but some of us just wanted to assert our ability to sing and demonstrate that we knew the piece. That was just part of the fun, and all in the Christmas spirit, but not an ingredient of quality. At the conclusion we joined the audience in giving ourselves a standing ovation as we were all pleased with our effort.

Jim and I had very much enjoyed ourselves and drove home feeling good about the season and the Santa Barbara community that could be home to such an amiable musical event. I asked him if he had ever sung the piece before and he replied that he had not. I pondered the labor of all my lessons, practice tapes, rehearsals, and effort to sing the famous *Messiah* and wondered at his courage and musicality to just go ahead and sing. But, surely, any way it is performed, a rousing performance of the *Messiah* is the best way to kindle the Christmas spirit.

* * *

The Los Angeles Master Chorale also offers an annual welcome-to-all *Messiah* with their orchestra, soloists, and conductor Grant Gershon at the famous Walt Disney Concert Hall. More than two-thousand singers from Southern California buy tickets and converge for a night of massed choral work in the grandest style. Kate and I agreed to have a night out in Los Angeles and join the famous event.

We arrived early, as we were concerned about the commuter

traffic, but were in plenty of time to enjoy dinner at the beautiful Disney Hall and relax before the concert. A chance meeting in the parking lot led to our joining six members of the St. Mathew's Episcopal Church of Pacific Palisades, who were out for a night of *Messiah*. These singers were typical of the audience who had pulled out their music scores for years with the Master Chorale and were excited about joining a couple of thousand others to make great music. An usher commented that the entrance lobby noise level of this audience was easily twice the volume of a philharmonic concert. People were up for the evening.

On this night, we sat according to our reserved seats—not in the accustomed voice sections—and we were front and center; but I was lonely without a bass within hearing and Kate regretted an empty seat without a singing companion. We warmed up with the famous "Hallelujah Chorus" and I had the lonely feeling of singing a solo in a group of sopranos and altos. One tenor sat in front of me, but the two of us probably only confused each other. After intermission, Kate allowed me to join our new Episcopal friends, and I enjoyed teaming up with another bass. The sound was somewhat ragged with disparate and varied talents coming from all directions, but what was lost in precision, gained in enthusiasm and impact.

This was a *Messiah* as the angels might sing. Our conductor, Greg Gershon, led us with introductory remarks for each section, sweeping arm and hand gestures, and facial expressions of encouragement. We could hear that some had trained voices, knew their score, and were up for leadership. One man, however, sitting behind us in the second half, had no sense of pitch whatsoever, and came in loudly once, only to draw a pointed grimace from a soprano neighbor who turned around to him with disdain. Once again, the pleasure of a little training paid off to those who could keep up and join in the fun with confidence.

The two sing-a-long *Messiah*s taught me some lessons. One can enjoy singing on a number of levels, and find great satisfaction in participating in a great work without the trouble of training and rehearsals needed for a performing choral group. There is, however, a substantial difference between a trained, auditioned, rehearsed, and properly directed chorus, and a volunteer crowd larking with a familiar piece of music. The first is art, and the second is community fun. On both nights our beat lagged behind the conductor, despite his efforts to pump us back up to speed by vigorously waving his arms. Our entrances were hesitant, and our singing clearly wavered during the more difficult parts, only to surge back up to volume during the familiar melodic phrases. If our tone came out on the right note, it was probably because of compensating errors and not a unity of purpose. That is not to say that we were not impressive choruses in our way, and were very much enjoyed by those in the audiences.

I also learned that, although I now had years of training, had sung the *Messiah* twice in concert and knew the rhythm, notes, and words almost by memory, my singing has limitations. In both sing-a-longs, I had tried to sing out and, I am ashamed to say, lead my neighbors with my hard-won skills. I over-sang and made many mistakes in my enthusiasm to contribute. I somewhat realized what was happening and tried to rein myself in and sing at my normal range and volume, only to give in to the temptation to fill the gaps and help others with leadership I did not possess. The day after my Santa Barbara sing-a-long, I wound up with a sore throat, a sure sign that I had over-sung, and quantity had very much overshadowed quality.

For all that, I look forward to future sing-a-longs with pleasurable anticipation. The warmth of the season is increased by vocalizing with neighbors, and the joy of Christmas is certainly enhanced by the shared music.

Chapter Fourteen

VERDI MOMENTS

● ● ●

CONTEMPORARY POLITICAL commentators and pundits love to moan and groan about the current lack of civility in American politics, as though our squabbles are exceptional. This only shows that they do not know history or understand the potentials of political incivility.

Giuseppe Verdi lived and composed in the mid-1800s, during the national Italian struggle to unify the country. At that time, his country was divided into a number of separate entities, including a large northern area occupied by the Austrian empire. There was lethal strife between the nationalists who wanted to throw out the Austrians, abolish the other small states, and unify the country, and those who wanted to hold on to their existing fiefdoms. Verdi's music inspired many patriotic Italian nationalists who, in his honor, adopted a unique rallying cry during their insurrections.

When nationalists shouted, "Viva Verdi!" at musical events and political rallies, they really were saying an acronym for their battle cry, *"Viva Vittorio Emanuele Re d'Italia"* or, translated, "Long Live Victorio Emanuel King of Italy," whom they wanted as ruler of their united country.

Verdi was never directly implicated during these dangerous times, called the "Risorgimento," but he was certainly sympathetic to, and involved with, the cause of Italian unification. Justice was very rough in those days, and he was fortunate to escape prison, or worse. Somehow, the authorities never caught on to his role and, although he remained independent of the fighting and was careful with public statements, his music certainly reflected the drama and struggles of the period, as great music often inspires emotions in dangerous times.

Verdi's music continued to be inspirational in other periods of history. During the Nazi regime, Jews and other designated enemies of the state were arrested and sent to prison camps. During that terrible time in the Czech Republic, a Gestapo prison called "Theresienstadt" served as propaganda to convince the world that such prison institutions were actually benevolent "resettlement" camps. Accordingly, the Nazis encouraged artistic programs in the prison to parade before visiting diplomats and Red Cross representatives. The truth was monstrously different.

As the camp contained many musicians, one of the infamous demonstration programs was a performance of Verdi's Requiem by inmate musicians and singers. This tragic story can best be illustrated by a letter from a Santa Barbara neighbor, Norman Jaffe, published in the *Santa Barbara News-Press*. He had heard about the planned Choral Society concert, and his letter of May 10, 2009, telling of his sad family history, including the performance of this piece of music, is quoted here in full to illustrate the dimensions of music:

"Dear Editor: An ad in the News Press titled '*Requiem*'—a commemorative concert to be performed by the Santa Barbara Choral Society and orchestra on May 16 & 17 in remembrance of the prisoners of Terezin'—brought back memories of a most frightening time of my youth in Dresden, Germany 1942.

"I was 18 years old, the son of an upper middle class Jewish family. My mother was an opera singer and pianist who also sang on the stage of Dresden's Semper Opera House; my father, the owner of a three-story furniture department store.

"On July 28, 1942, at the break of dawn, violent banging, knocking and shouts at our front door awoke us. 'Aufmachen! Open at once!' Gestapo agents yelled and forced themselves into my parents' bedroom, grabbing my father and ordering my mother from their bed, barking at them to be dressed in five minutes....

"My parents were forced up onto a waiting truck. Mother's last words to me were: 'See you in Heaven.' As the truck pulled away, I realized I had become an orphan. Returning to our rooms, I slid into my parent's bed still warm from their bodies and cried.

"This was transport of elderly Jews who were considered worthless to the Nazis for slave labor. My orders were to report to a slave labor camp called Hellerberg for the Nazi defense industry working on time bomb-clock movements administered by Zeiss Ikon GmbH.

"One day a postcard arrived from mother. The card face said, 'beautiful Theresienstadt (Terezin.)' Written on the other side, she said: 'Stay strong! Performing opera for SS Officers. Father died. Love the flowers here. We will be together again. Love, Mother.'

"In 1990 after the reunification of Germany, I visited Dresden. We decided to visit Prague, a two hour drive away. Along the way, we noticed a huge parking lot, an impressive building and many people. Our curiosity made us stop. We found ourselves on holy ground.

"We entered what was formerly a garrison town with rows of grave markers honoring Czeck freedom fighters. Reaching the entrance gate we were shocked to be told that we were in the former Jewish ghetto of Theresienstadt, where my parents had been taken in 1942. It was a prisoner collection camp for those to be sent to Auschwitz. To the outside world, it was presented as a model cultural oasis, for musicians, singers, actors, artists, writers, etc....

"The archives, neatly printed, showed us my parent's names, birth dates, date of transport—and destiny. My father was shot Nov. 1, 1942. My mother was transported by cattle car to Auschwitz on Jan. 29. In March of 1943, she, known as prisoner 104954 arrived in Auschwitz.

"Terezin, also known as an ancient fortress, was liberated by Soviet forces in May, 1945. Verdi's *Requiem* will be performed May 17 in Terezin, in remembrance of the prisoners who lived and died there.

"This dedication is for my mother, Margarethe Flasch Jaffe."

This letter dramatically retold the history of one of our neighbors whose mother was a singing performer in that pathetic, and inspired, prison camp production of the *Requiem*. Imagine the musicians living in fear of death, but singing the immortal words of freedom and liberation contained in the Requiem Mass. Imagine the Nazis, including the arch-executioner Colonel Adolf Eichmann and visiting dignitaries, sitting in the audience. To the singers it was a moment of inspiration, despair, and defiance. To the Nazis it was a moment of humorous irony, because they knew there were secret plans to transport the prisoners to death camps.

The *Requiem*, a Mass for the dead, was first performed in 1874 in memory of the famous Italian writer and poet, Alessandro Manzoni, who was a close friend of Verdi's. The Mass includes moving and dramatic passages that convey emotions of longing for deliverance and God's mercy. The opening phrases are sung *sotto voce,* or barely audible but with energy and drama:

"*Requiem*! *Requiem aeternam. Donna eis requiem Domine. Et lux perpetua luceat eis!*"

"Eternal rest give to them, O Lord; and let perpetual light shine upon them!"

And after dramatic and soaring passages describing the days of terrible rage and moving pleas for mercy and forgiveness, the music finally concludes with a plea, sung with hushed intensity:

"*Libera me, Domine, de morte aeterna, in die illa tremenda!*"

"Deliver me, Oh, Lord, from everlasting death, on that dreadful day!"

When the great musical masterpiece concludes with this somber and powerful final phrase, the audience usually sits in silence before acknowledging the performance, in our case, with a standing ovation.

As we rehearsed for the performance, scheduled for May 16 and 17, 2009, our Santa Barbara Choral Society discovered the amazing and unplanned coincidence that our performance would fall on the exact anniversary day of the liberation of the Terezin prison camp in 1945. After reading the history of the camp and speaking with descendants of internees, we unanimously decided to dedicate the performance to the prisoners.

Our concert began without a curtain raising or conductor's and soloists' entrance, but rather with a silent procession to our places and a solemn spoken message to the audience relating the concentration camp story and our dedication of the concert to the inmates. The gradual raising of the lights, the quiet opening chords of the orchestra, and almost whispered words of the chorus initiated a truly emotional and inspired performance for all of us. We paused only briefly in the middle of the piece, and then continued with no intermission. The orchestra, singers, and audience shared a moving and historical musical moment.

The Society invited Norman Jaffe, author of the above letter, to attend our dress rehearsal privately, in sympathy with his feelings. We could only imagine the thoughts and emotions in his mind as we sang the words his mother had sung. The concert was the most dramatic experience of my singing career; it was a privilege to feel at one with those prisoners who sang the same notes, far removed from the comfort and safety of Santa Barbara. I could not help but think about Norman Jaffe's mother who performed the piece, hoping to change the evil minds of the Nazis, but, more realistically, as an affirmation of her art and her life.

Verdi's *Requiem* is composed in a grand, operatic style. Indeed, the score calls for full orchestra, four soloists, and large choir. The singers move from hushed-silent pianissimo, to full-voice fortissimo. The music is beautifully lyrical and a joy to sing, and engenders grand emotions in both performers and audience. Somehow, in my short singing career, the piece continues to be an inspiration and source of amazing experiences.

*　*　*

During our 2010 London fall visit, while searching for Evensongs around the country, Kate and I visited Gloucester Cathedral, one of the heritage beauties of England, which had risen from a Benedictine monastery in 1540. Evensongs have been held there every day since its foundation. We were about three hours early and intended to tour the Cathedral and then the town before the service. To our good fortune, as we peered into the great structure, we stumbled on the Gloucester Choral Society and the English Symphony Orchestra about to hold a dress rehearsal for a concert the next day and, of all things, they were singing the Verdi *Requiem*.

We helped ourselves to seats and settled in the vast and beautiful nave, practically by ourselves, pretending to belong to the organization. The chorus and orchestra sailed into Verdi with spirit from bleachers constructed above the altar space. The people looked and sounded much like our Santa Barbara Choral Society, and we thoroughly enjoyed our private concert. Afterwards, we mingled with some singers in a medieval vaulted tearoom off the old monastery cloister and wished them a splendid performance, which I am confident came off well.

* * *

On another trip, in 2009, in order to make plane connections, Kate and I were staying overnight in Amsterdam. After checking into our hotel, we asked the concierge if there was anything interesting going on in town, particularly in the music scene. She searched the computer and said, "Well, there is some kind of performance of Verdi's *Requiem* at the Concertgebouw." This is the famous grand concert hall of Amsterdam and we learned she had spoken correctly: It was some kind of *Requiem*!

We discovered on arriving at the hall that all the serious choruses in Holland had been practicing for a year to combine into one single grand performance on that night. The entire ground floor audience section was occupied by over eight- hundred chorus members. A full orchestra and four excellent soloists were accompanied by this mass of voices. To accommodate the crowd of singers, two additional sub-conductors stood on each side, relaying direction to the side seats. We sat with the audience in the balconies, surrounding this musical tidal wave, in seats above the orchestra and facing the singers. We reveled in the Dutch vocal might.

During the long intermission, many of the happy chorus members repaired to the bar and we mingled with some of the basses who hailed from a chorus in Rotterdam. They spoke excellent English and were pleased to visit with a couple from California.

Many in the American press and intelligentsia talk about how our country is despised abroad. In my travels I have never found that to be the case, and in fact, quite the opposite. The Rotterdam singers' mood was pride and pleasure in the impressive concert, and they were making a great evening of it. I tried to promote a singer's seat in their section, but all were taken, and they probably would rather have had Kate join them anyway.

* * *

When Kate and I planned a three-month trade of our home in California for some friends' apartment in London in 2010, the scheme hinged on an audition and acceptance by an accomplished chorus in England. After a good amount of searching, I decided to try for an organization called "The London Chorus," because of their reputation, and also because their fall concert would include Verdi's *Requiem*. Without telling any friends, in case of failure, I traveled to London to face an audition.

This time I was required to appear alone for the musical director, and do the usual tests I had experienced for the Santa Barbara Choral Society and, in addition, sing a solo piece of my selection. I have never intended nor aspired to sing solo, except when our congregation holds a Christmas pageant and I am forced to perform a wise man part from the hymn, "We Three Kings." In my recent singing days, I have been asked to do the occasional event-opening National Anthem, but have never accepted. I cringe and fume when hearing most renditions of that traditional patriotic piece. They tend to be overly dramatic and contain some truly creative pitches and rhythms; but like most armchair quarterbacks, I have kept my participation to complaining. Solos will never be for me, but in this audition, I bravely chose a simple and beautiful Italian song, composed by Giuseppe Giodani in the 1700s, "Caro Mio Ben." For preparation, two singing teachers, Rose Knoles and Ken Ryals taught me the song and drilled me a hundred times, and I sang it to myself hundreds more. This well-known piece must have served thousands of applicants over the generations, and it served me successfully in London.

After what I thought was an acceptable rendition for the London Chorus director, Ronald Corp, this friendly and talented man instructed me on three improvements I could make in singing the piece. He explained that the musical dynamics, the volume and emphasis in my voice bringing out the beauty and meaning of the piece, were lacking, and my rendition was too flat. He pointed out that I was clearly anticipating the high notes and needed to relax. He advised me to plan my breathing, to give full support to all my notes. He then welcomed me as a member of the Chorus bass section. I sang a private "Hallelujah." I knew if they would take me, they surely would—and did—accept Kate, and our fall in London was secured.

The Verdi performance by the London Chorus was to be in December 2010, at the end of our London visit. The Royal Orchestra Society, the premier amateur symphony in England, was producing the concert and had invited the London Chorus to perform as vocalists. Conductor Orlando Jopling led this impressive assemblage in a huge church, St. John's Smith Square. The stage was only large enough for the orchestra, so the chorus was divided, with half sitting on each side of the high balcony overlooking the musicians. I secured a perfect seat against the wall, directly overlooking the conductor, facing the sopranos across the stage space, and similarly overlooking the orchestra from the other side. From my perch the acoustics were somewhat strange, and I seemed to sing a lonely voice into open second-floor atmosphere; but my friends in the audience heard a beautiful blend of sound, so the arrangement functioned well.

Just to make the experience complete, I witnessed an event when securing tickets for friends before the concert that was reminiscent of the Verdi *Risorgimento* demonstrations. When I walked out from the church and down the street from Parliament House, there was a large demonstration, bordering on riot. Angry students were staging a day of protest against increases in fees, and twenty thousand or more were massed on the road. Most of the noise came from the direction of Parliament, so I walked through the crowd in that direction. Had I turned the other way, I would have been in the middle of rioting, fighting, arrests, and the trashing of the Conservative Party headquarters by the most militant of the students. As it was, I only watched drumming, chanting, and milling, and had some friendly conversations with young students who wanted to know all about higher education in California. In the midst of my preparation for a splendid concert there was another world of riots and political unrest, but I was preoccupied with my musical dreams come true; the protesters gave me a sympathetic pass, probably because my head was in the Verdi clouds.

The concert was sold out and well received. Some English friends and a few of Kate's family showed up to cheer us on. They had all known me in former business days in England when singing was the furthest thing from my life, and were now somewhat nonplussed to see the old me flailing away in the London Chorus. But such is life, and we all enjoyed a glass of wine in the church crypt after the concert, toasting a couple of old dogs learning new tricks. Singing with these good people was pleasure enough, but while there we were recruited for another performance of the *Requiem* that became one of our great singing experiences.

* * *

The modern Bart's Choir is one of the largest singing organizations in England, having evolved from a group of Bart's Hospital singing nurses into a major performing group. Their purpose is to promote choral singing and requires from their singers, who are accepted without audition, only enthusiasm and a willingness to work. Kate and I were asked to join them for the *Requiem* on the strength of our acceptance by the London Chorus and, as we had little idea what we were getting ourselves into, I went to one of their rehearsals in a huge church in downtown London to scout the group. I arrived late and found a mass of singers— with the sopranos and altos sitting in the pews and, facing them from the altar and choir area, a crowd of tenors and basses.

The rehearsal had begun and I was forced to thread my way up into the very back of the choir area, standing well above the conductor, among total strangers. The bass section included characters of all ages and abilities singing out with a will. I joined in with confidence, as I had sung the piece before and was rehearsing the *Requiem* with the London Chorus. At the break, I simply signed on with the bass section organizer and paid my thirty-five-pounds dues to become a member of the throng. I soon came to thoroughly enjoy this delightful organization that sang with enthusiasm and with a high quality. In my section, I tried to filter myself among those who had the best voices, as I gradually discovered the details of the concert to come.

Kate came along to the following week's rehearsal and we almost suffered a major setback in our English tour, solved only by ignoring the problem. Kate had arrived to the chorus one week later than I, and only a few rehearsals were scheduled before the performance, so she was required to audition to determine if she knew the piece. Unfortunately, she had learned the alto part in

Santa Barbara, but was now relearning the second soprano part for the London Chorus and wanted to sing the same with Bart's. After rehearsal, Kate auditioned with a tired pianist and an impatient conductor, and in dim light. The conductor directed her to the most difficult section in the entire piece, the "Sanctus", and she had to start off solo. Kate became flustered with the unfamiliar soprano line; things did not go well, and she did not pass.

We repaired to a pub in confusion and, over a glass of wine, agonized about what to do next. I would not sing without her and we both wanted to do the concert. Kate knew she was at least as good as the people she had sung with that night and, with practice, could handle the part without difficulty. At length, we decided to ignore the rejection, as the conductor did not know her and we hoped he would forget the audition. If she were discovered, she would say she was only waiting for me to finish rehearsal. As it turned out, the second soprano section was delighted to have her, she stayed on the roster, received a performer's pass, and had a splendid concert. If the conductor had only known her true abilities, doubtless he would have been pleased also.

We were scheduled to sing at the Royal Albert Hall with the Royal Philharmonic Orchestra and more than four-hundred singers. The Royal Albert Hall is the premier music performance venue in England, except, possibly, the Royal Opera House. Queen Victoria built the architectural masterpiece and dedicated the impressive building to the memory of her deceased husband, Prince Albert, in 1871. The building is oval shaped with a round roof, and has sound baffles in the huge ceiling to improve acoustics. The materials are red brick and light red blocks supporting a steel-framed oval roof. The hall holds fifty-five hundred, although it has contained up to nine thousand for special occasions. With our huge chorus taking up the seats surrounding the orchestra, Bart's had five thousand tickets to sell. The Bart's Chorus president happily told us at dress rehearsal that they were almost sold out and were actually making a profit on the concert! We planned to take that experience back and report it to Santa Barbara.

Our talented conductor, Ivor Setterfield, rehearsed us with enthusiasm and exhibited a range of emotions from sarcasm to inspirational praise. He was clearly in charge and knew what he wanted, and how to make us give it to him. Fortunately for us basses, he focused most of his attention on the altos and sopranos who were fundamentally sound, but occasionally experienced lapses and required herding. The tenors had some real talent, but tended to show off and sound off, although they did add energy and substance to the music. It is hard to evaluate a chorus of more than four-hundred singers, but real quality was emerging from the crowded rehearsal space. An excitement grew within the basses and, I believe, all of the sections, that we would have a very credible concert. Basses tend to be older guys, and there was a considerable range of talent in our section, from those with true ability, to those more given to quiet mumbling. Fortunately, the former emerged and produced quality sound and volume to hold up the bass part.

I had a moment of truth in one of our final rehearsals. We met temporarily in a new hall, rented for an extra Saturday rehearsal the week before the concert. There was considerable shuffling of chairs and sections, and the basses were asked to form in a wedge leading directly to the conductor. I sat in the second row, very much under the conductor's gaze, next to one of the better bass voices. When the milling about had calmed down, we realized that we two were totally surrounded by tenors, and the nearest friendly basses were well behind us. There was no possibility of rearranging, so we grew where planted and managed quite well holding our lower notes in a sea of tenors. However, there is one lonely and exposed moment for the basses when, after the chorus sings mezzo forte (medium strength) "*sal va me*" (save me!), there is dramatic pause, and then the basses enter by themselves with "*sal va me*" at pianissimo (very quiet, but with energy.) Our opening note was an E, and the second note was a C, which is at the upper end of the bass range, particularly when sung quietly. My neighbor informed me that he had some problems hitting the high note, which almost destroyed my own questionable confidence.

The conductor, leading from right in front of us, decided to go over that particular section, starting with the basses. In the event, I hit the note and brought my neighbor along as well. We repeated, and I hit it again. Finally, the conductor brought in everybody and we were right on once more for the little solo section. The conductor was satisfied and moved on, and I fought down the urge to stand up and shout, "We did it!" That challenging moment reinforced my assurance in my brief singing career. I felt I had reached a level I never believed possible and, whether truly deserved or not, I continued on with new confidence.

The dress rehearsal was on the afternoon of the concert and we proudly entered the famous Royal Albert Hall, admitted by our performers' passes. Kate, still hiding from the conductor's gaze, was first ushered many rows up where vertigo abounded, and the London Philharmonic Orchestra sat below as a distant presence. Then, fortunately, an assistant conductor decided more second sopranos were needed up front, and she happily settled into a lower and center seat.

The conductor had rightly decided that four-hundred-plus voices would be too loud singing as a full chorus when a soloist was featured. Accordingly for those primarily solo moments, he chose a group from each section to sing the chorus parts. I was fortunate to be in the bass group singing the softer music behind the soloists. In this section of voices, I found myself standing in the front row, singing with competent voices, and with an excellent view of the conductor. I could not believe the moment. I was in the front row, just behind the Royal Philharmonic Orchestra in the Royal Albert Hall, singing the Verdi *Requiem* that I knew and loved. That experience brought me to a place of artistic euphoria from which I shall probably never recover.

For the performance, we took our seats early, as four-hundred singers could not easily be formally ushered in. We watched the audience take their seats with the satisfaction of noting a nearly full house. The moment arrived and the low intense notes led us into the magic world of Verdi. The concert was almost flawless and the four-hundred-plus voices and accomplished orchestra matched every bit of drama in the piece from a hushed murmur to a full-voice crescendo. There is a loud bass drum part where percussionists have been known to thrust the padded drumstick through the drum's skin. We were standing directly behind the drum section, and answered the wham of the drum with deep-throated voices, giving as good as we got.

The audience gave the performance a great ovation, although the English custom is not to stand. When the chorus was acknowledged there was noticeable rise in the applause, and I could only imagine the audience was heavily populated with singers' family and friends. Kate's brother, John, who knew that I could never aspire to do what I had just accomplished, attended, and even he was impressed.

From time to time I have been asked what was my favorite piece to sing. This reminds me of the question about one's favorite wine. I answer the latter question by replying that this would depend on the climate, food, mood, and other factors that bring a preferred wine to mind. But if one were stuck on a desert island with many food options and was forced to choose only one wine for the year, what would that wine be? I would want a red burgundy called, "La Tache." The same applies to music. If I were locked in a concert hall for a year with a great chorus and orchestra, but could sing only one piece of music, I would want it to be Verdi's *Requiem*.

The variety of performances of Verdi's *Requiem* in history and around the world illustrates the importance and impact of choral singing beyond the artistic form. The drama, communal expression, and symbolism of choral music conveys a wide variety of involvement with world occasions.

Chapter Fifteen

BEATLES PREMIER

● ● ●

IN THE LATE SIXTIES my career as a tire executive took our family to London where we lived down the street from a family of good neighbors named George and Judy Martin. George Martin was pleasant, laid-back company, and we became friends, although the significance of what he did and who he was did not mean much to us at first. Subsequently, I came to understand that he was the genius behind the Beatles' music and produced most of their hits over the years. When we left England in 1972 we kept in touch and, somewhere in the mid-seventies, George visited our ranch in the Santa Ynez Valley.

George was in California to present a film producer with an original composition for an upcoming production called *The Mission*. He played the tape for us, including a choral piece entitled "Mission Chorales" that sounded particularly beautiful and remained in my mind. As it turned out, his compositions were not used because the original producer sold his script and movie rights to another producer who used different music. Of course, I never dreamed I would meet "Mission Chorales" again.

In 2008 we saw George in Los Angeles where he was receiving a Grammy Award for producing the Cirque de Soleil show *Love* in Las Vegas. I asked him what became of that choral piece I had once heard. He replied, "Nothing." That seemed a great waste, and I asked him where it was. He replied that it was in his drawer and had never been produced or released in any form. I asked him if he would ever want it to be performed, and he said he would very much like to hear the long-lost piece. He knew that I had begun singing with the Choral Society, and when I asked him if we could sing it, he agreed! I did not know the extent of what I had asked, although he did.

The gift of a world premier of Sir George Martin's composition would necessarily cause him a good deal of work to complete for an orchestra and choral performance, and was no light undertaking. But he thought it would be fun to do, and generously gave us the opportunity for the price of a plane ticket to visit the premier performance. "Generous" was an understatement because, in his eighties, with serious hearing and health problems, and with incredible demands on his time and talent, George was about to give a treasure to the Santa Barbara Choral Society. The Society began to plan for the event a few months away.

To add another work and fill out the evening program, the Society agreed on a collaboration with State Street Ballet, a very accomplished and talented local company that performs nationally. They would create a ballet, based on the Beatles' themes, to be performed with the Society singing the background music on the same program with "Mission Chorales." We had months to go before the scheduled performance, but there was much to do.

George worked on the "Mission Chorales," which had lain unfinished for more than thirty years, and set the music to four-part choral harmony with orchestra. Simultaneously, we needed to complete the music and choreography for the ballet, also on the evening program. For this, Beatles' themes were rearranged and set to choral music by Steve Dombek, a member of our Society, while a New York choreographer, William Soleau, conceived an entirely new full-length story set for ballet dancing.

We had previously worked with the ballet company the year before, singing Carl Orff's famous piece Camina Burana, a dynamic and exciting series of songs based on medieval poems and stories. The same Beatles' production choreographer, William Soleau, created a dramatic ballet storyline and dance set with a medieval theme for the Carmina music. We were at that time optimistic about the idea of a collaboration between the chorus and ballet, even if initially we did not know what to expect.

Carmina Burana was the first collaboration between our Choral Society and the State Street Ballet, or any other ballet, and everyone was curious when our two organizations first rehearsed together. Kate was very much at home, back in the ballet world, but few in the chorus had ever shared the stage with ballet dancers, and the dancers had never experienced a hundred singers standing behind them. The young beautifuls on the floor and we singers on the risers eyed one another as the ballet dancers stretched and we warmed up our voices. Our director admonished the basses and tenors to keep our eyes on her baton and direction and not the dancers; but in the early rehearsals there was some wandering attention and missed downbeats when the dancers posed and leaped. The basses would not have been able to produce an acceptable deep resonance if they had no interest in those long-legged beauties.

In the previous season the dramatic music and hauntingly

beautiful *Carmina Burana* ballet had been a sellout and very popular with the audience community. Our collaboration turned out to be a great success and gave us the confidence to undertake the Beatles ballet a year later.

We all looked forward to collaborating again with the ballet people, and their dancing to another original ballet, this time set to Beatles' music. Both organizations rehearsed at length separately, and then together, with the added excitement that George had decided to conduct the "Mission Chorales" personally; we wanted to be well prepared for him. The prestige of both a George Martin premier and one conducted by the composer himself created a buzz in Santa Barbara and challenge to dancers and singers to be up to the occasion. The rehearsals seemed to go well for both the "Mission Chorales" and the ballet, entitled "Love, Love, Love!" The songs to be used with the fascinating Beatles' rhythms and lyrics were: "Help"; "Something"; "Here, There and Everywhere"; "For No One"; "The Word"; "In My Life"; and, of course, "All You Need Is Love." At length we were very ready for the composer to arrive.

George and Judy flew in to stay with us a few days before the concert. It was a great reunion. George is a tall man, who resembles an ambassador, bishop, or philosophy professor, rather than a musician famous for producing the Beatles. He is the most universally pleasant individual anyone could meet, and absolutely without the pride of place his career would warrant. His gentle manner, smile, and conservative British ways immediately won over everyone. Judy is the perfect English lady with her open, gracious, and no-nonsense personality. We arranged for a driver to take George back and forth for his part of the rehearsal, to preserve his energy in every way possible. He had all the musicians in the palm of his hand when he stood in front of the orchestra and chorus for his first rehearsal, smiled and said, "Good evening. I am glad to be here, and this is going to be fun," Although his health had left him somewhat frail, his conducting was vigorous, and straightforward; his expressions and small gestures told us all we needed to know.

Our performance could only be appropriately accommodated at the Granada Performing Arts Center and, on opening night, we warmed up in a studio, hidden in the basement, with more than the usual excitement. Word filtered from the front of the house that we had a sell-out, and there were people outside looking for anyone with an extra ticket. The music is the same, and the performance should be the same, to a small audience, but somehow when the theater is packed, adrenalin starts to flow and the vocal batteries go to full charge.

George Martin introduced the "Chorales" to the audience, describing the scene in the jungles of Brazil. He explained how a party of Jesuit missionaries, canoeing up a river in the deep jungle, came upon a large group of tribal warriors standing on the bank, viewing Europeans for the first time. The music begins with threatening, guttural war challenges from the Indians. The missionaries reply in the only way they could think of—by singing an oratorio, the Mission Chorales. It was a short, beautifully full piece, with soaring chorus sections, an oboe solo, and a haunting soprano section representing a choir boy singing. After hearing George Martin describe the scene we were even more excited to sing the music.

The piece began with the threatening cries of the Indians: "Shhhhh! Sheeka, Sheeka, Sheeka! Sheeka, Sheeka, Sheeka! Uha! OO! A! Chumba, Chumba, Chumba! Tika, Ti-Ti-Ka, Ti-Ka-Tik! Uhah!" These eighteen measures carried on with many variations of rhythm, written differently for each section. We soon understood that singing in Latin, German, or French, would be easier than mastering these complex beats in made-up Amazon Indian. But relief came in the missionary reply, a lyrical "Hosanna in Excelsis Deo" that led us into the familiar ground of the oratorio. There followed an all-too-brief, but dramatic and harmonious chorus, vocal solo, and instrumental tour de force ending with *Et in nomine tuo levabo manus meus, Allelulia!"* or, "And in Your name lift up my hands, Hallelujah!" The work that had rested for years came alive, and the audience also came alive with cheers for a very pleased George Martin.

George and Judy sat in the audience while Jo Anne Wassserman conducted us in the "Love, Love, Love!" ballet. He told me later that he experienced great pleasure in hearing the familiar music set to a full-length ballet so well. The music was a serious variation of familiar Beatles' tunes, and the State Street Ballet presented a dramatic and meaningful '60s storyline that moved both chorus and audience.

Each performance has its own rewards, and this one, as well as being beautiful music and dance, was an exhilarating reminiscence of past songs in the ballet as well as the pleasure of hearing the "Mission Chorales" for the first time. The thrill of being conducted by such an icon of the music world and singing his premier was an historic moment in all our careers. It sounded splendid! And one could feel the audience excitement.

The cast party with the Martins and the ballet people was the best we ever had, with nostalgia and congratulations all around. I made sure all the ballerinas had a chance to flirt with the composer, which he appreciated. George and I had never expected that we would share the same stage in a musical production, but he took great delight in Kate's and my late-life career and passion to sing his music. The "Mission Chorales" has since been performed a number of times in England.

Chapter Sixteen

$\mathcal{Y}$OUNG $\mathcal{V}$OICES

● ● ●

MANLY, MASCULINE DADS should not worry if their young sons have high, feminine voices. In time, these voices will change, and the young men will take their places in the tenor, baritone, and bass sections. Until that day when they lose their young sound, some of the best soprano soloists and section members have been boys with voices of a slightly different tone than girls and women, and with an excellent blending quality.

Members of the bass section take pride in their ability to hit low notes, and those individuals who are able to sing below a low E with a good blending tone are a prized commodity in any chorus. This bass quality comes to men as they age, and young boys can look forward to beards, bulk, and low voices in the future; meanwhile, they produce glorious high notes until this inevitable voice change. But they do not appreciate being called "sopranos," because those are girls; boys should be known as "trebles," a designation that defines a very special male singing status.

In wine terms, a female soprano sounds like the light, fruity, and delicious flavors of a glass of Riesling, made with the fresh, grapey quality we expect in America. This wine, with residual sugar content, will present a bright, voluptuous quality if it is well-produced from noble grapes. On the other hand, the European style dry Riesling, without the residual, natural sugar, will also present a luscious quality, but with an austerity reminiscent of a desert wind blowing in the wildflower season. The dry style is prized for its ability to blend with great cuisine. Likewise, the slight tonal edge in the texture of a treble boy's voice, like a great dry Riesling, adds an ethereal purity to choral music that blends into the heavier voice sections with a unique grace.

A well-trained young boy, with musicality and soaring high tone, is much appreciated in a number of the best church choirs in the world. In the 1700s such boys were sought after to add luster to the choirs in the noble courts of Europe, and sometimes virtually kidnapped from their families and communities to serve the boasting rights of princes and kings. This singing tradition survives in some choirs and a few exceptional schools in the world today, where the boys mostly perform in cathedral choirs when not on a performing tour.

The New York magazine recently rated the top 101 things to do in New York City. Forget the first forty and go to the forty-first: St. Thomas Church on Fifth Avenue and Fifty-Third St. for a sung service, particularly an Evensong. On most days at 5:30 p.m. there will be an Evensong held in the classic gothic church, a monument of spiritual peace and musical excellence firmly planted in the bustle of the city.

The heart of the service is the choir, which includes students from the St. Thomas Choir School. The school is the last surviving institution totally dedicated to choir training in America, and has a rigorous academic and musical program with many concerts, in addition to the church services. Any parent with a young musical son would do well to consider the splendid opportunity offered by this school, although the program requires a mature and well-motivated young individual.

Student applicants are sought from New York City and from around the country for the boarding school. Approximately eight boys are admitted each year with a maximum population of forty students. There are nine full-time and ten part-time teachers, and two school nurses, with many staff living with the boys in the large building around the corner from the church. Admittance will come only after musical and academic assessments, and a required overnight visit to the school to determine if the young boy is prepared for city life. Like the Marine Corps, Jesuit seminary, or Cordon Bleu Cooking School, if the boy buys the program there will be great success; but alternately, if the boy is unhappy in such a structured setting the application is best forgotten.

Boys can be given significant financial help from the school foundation, but they will be required to study, behave well, and sing in the boys choir. The school, on a busy New York street, has maintained its high standards and traditions since 1919. Those fortunate enough to be admitted and who graduate, go on to interesting and successful academic and life careers. By the eighth grade, many of the boys have had a change of voice which, of course, ends their soprano careers, and relegates them to other church and school activities. The voice change can be gradual or sudden; many boys resist the change and fight to maintain the high notes during a period of voice transition. Alternately, a startled choir director on a concert tour might be greeted at breakfast by a boyish baritone "Good morning" and there will be panic for lack of a treble voice in the section.

During the school year, when Evensong time nears, the boys will "crocodile" the few blocks from school to St. Thomas. Here they are combined with sixteen bass, tenor, and countertenor men to make up the church choir, famous through numerous recordings and world tours, and available to sing services for everyone who wanders into the church. The choir will perform around four-hundred separate pieces of church music each year, and these must be mastered and rehearsed rapidly. In the basement room the men and boys will go over the scheduled music for the evening and don their red robes with white collars prior to processing to the service.

I am fortunate to know Rev. Canon John Andrews, who had been chaplain to the Archbishop of Canterbury before becoming rector of St. Thomas, and is now rector emeritus. He arranged my tour of St. Thomas Choir School, and we walked the classes together. Each roomful of boys stood when we entered, shook hands, and told me what they were studying. The fifteen-story building houses some of the faculty, all of the students, and the headmaster, Rev. Charles Wallace. The classrooms are well-situated for the small sections, and all the dormitories and other amenities are contained in the building, including a short-court basketball facility. We were invited for tea and enjoyed a long discussion with three senior, eighth-grade boys who were as interested in me as I was in them, and very impressive conversationalists. I would be happy to have any grandson in the school.

After the visit, Rev. Andrews walked me down Fifth Avenue to the Evensong service. We sat in the choir stalls behind the singers and watched the hundred or so weekday congregation and tourists take their seats in the large nave. The choir quietly filed in and I noticed the focused expressions on the boys' faces. Immediately in front of us sat the youngest students who were not yet ready to sing in the choir. They occupied a choir bench, sitting quietly except when they almost lost their composure during the long Old

Testament lesson, earning a stern look from a senior boy. A full service program sheet had been passed to everyone outlining the entire schedule, including prelude, service, and anthem music.

The service began with a priest chanting, "O Lord open Thou our lips," and then the voices of the choir soared with the choral response, "And our mouths shall show forth Thy praise." Thank you, Archbishop Cranmer.

St. Thomas was familiar to us because my widowed father had been remarried in the church, and Kate had attended services during her ballet tours to America, because this was the closest church to her hotel. In fact, the traditional services in my country, so well carried out, had worked in my favor by convincing this young Church of England dancer that we were not all heathens. Sitting in the choir and experiencing Evensong, also reassured this California country boy that there was hope for the big, brash city of New York.

After the service, we walked out into the noisy street confusion and, as it was Rev. John Andrew's birthday, we celebrated at the renowned Le Perigord restaurant, which also must be on the list of 101 best New York visits. Here, we tested the similarity of choir boys' contribution of voices to an important bottle of dry Riesling blended with great food, and found my judgment to be sound.

There is no question that young boys experience the excitement of music. Years ago I was invited, with my nine-year-old son Andrew, to a home football game at the University of Southern California. Football is a religion there, and we were in for a rare experience as guests of Ron Orr, then chair of the Alumni Association. In our special garden reception before the game, there was a magical moment when the famous USC Band paraded on the steps above the alumni and played fight songs. Games have been won on the strength of the two dozen trumpets and phalanx of trombones blasting minor keys, and the uniformed marching band gave us the full bore. I was holding Andrew on my shoulders for a good view, and the remembrance of the musical impact gives us both chills to this day. As the brass blared he kicked me and pounded my head, yelling, "Daddy, I want to go to college here!" Kids dig the spirit of music and convey that emotion.

As long as there have been ancient temples—long before Jesus walked the earth—singing and chanting, accompanied by young boys, has moved the spirits of worshipers. It is monstrous that early school kids are taught only nursery rhyme songs in school when they are capable of performing Bach oratorios or Mozart Masses. Insisting that one's children learn challenging music and perform as well as possible is good for the child, and certainly better for the listening world. The most famous example of this capability is the Vienna Boys Choir School.

The tenor section leader of our Berkshire Festival Chorus in Salzburg, Oliver Stech, was a choirmaster at the Vienna Boys Choir School and kindly invited us to visit the school and attend one of his classes. The choir is actually four choirs, regularly trained and maintained in the school. Boys are assessed, auditioned, and admitted to the school to become a member of one of the choirs; they will perform and train with that group of twenty-five. Each year, graduates will leave to provide spaces for new students to take their place in the individual choir groupings.

The various school choirs have been singing in the Austrian Imperial Chapel since the 1600s. The boys were well treated and the pride of the royal family, but now the Emperor and Imperial Court have long departed, replaced by dignitaries and tourists from around the world who come to the well-maintained Royal Chapel to hear the choir. The four school choirs rotate singing duties, and a boy might participate in eighty to a hundred concerts each year, with one of the choirs always on a tour somewhere in the world. Our host's class had just suffered a cancellation of their trip to Japan, due to the tsunami disaster, but were preparing for a South American tour in a few months.

The school is in a large nineteenth-century building with high ceilings and huge windows and doors. The marble staircases echoed with the sound of young boys dashing to classes. There were old and new pictures of choirboys posing by monuments around the world and with heads of state. We found our way to a large classroom with a semicircle of raised seats and music stands for the boys and, of course, a grand piano. We sat in the front with another couple, also guests, and the boys gave us curious English hellos, although they mostly spoke German. They were polite, but energetic, with the shaggy clothes and mussed hair typical of schoolboys the world over.

Oliver Stech waved them to silence and warmed up their voices with scales and exercises. We noticed some fidgeting, private jokes, and looks typical of any schoolboy. The kids appeared to be as natural as any boys might be shooting hoops on a basketball court or standing around eating ice cream cones—except they were producing stunning sounds with their voices. After the warm-up, Oliver told them to turn to page forty-two, measure seventy-five of the Haydn Mass they were preparing, and with the same ease and natural demeanor, they soared into the music. The twenty-five boys may or may not have been showing off for visitors, but their singing was amazing. We knew that these kids were bound for the stages of the world, and the world would be lucky to hear them.

The life of a young boy boarding at a choir school is not easy, but it is rewarding in later life, and certainly enjoyable for those who appreciate the music. Hopefully, parents of talented children will continue to consider the musical option.

Chapter Seventeen

$\mathcal{P}$ETER AND $\mathcal{P}$AUL

• • •

PETER WAS ONE of Jesus' Twelve Apostles, a fisherman from Galilee, who left an extensive record in cities of the Roman world, and finally became Bishop of Rome. Paul never knew Jesus, but was converted to believe in Him and became perhaps the most famous and influential Christian missionary, authoring many letters of the New Testament. The two Cathedrals, named for the saints, St. Peter's in Rome, and St. Paul's in England, were to be the scenes of important experiences for Kate and me—one extraordinary and one frustrating.

The truth about Rome traffic is that it is bad, unless you are anxious about being somewhere important and behind schedule, and then it is really bad! The two buses carrying our Santa Barbara Choral Society to St. Peter's Basilica for our engagement to sing at the five o'clock Mass were scheduled to arrive early, except for the snarls, hold-ups, horns, and shaking fists that slowed us to a crawl.

We were at last delivered onto the famous acres of piazza, surrounded by colonnades, before the immense historic building that immediately reduced us all in size as we trotted toward the giant basilica. A long line for security inspection held us up again, until finally admitting our chorus into the vast edifice where we became lost among thousands of the faithful and visiting tourists. At last our sixty-five singers were met by a guide who reassured us that we were in plenty of time, and our anxiety was replaced with a sense of the enormity of where we were and what we were about to do. We were singing where St. Peter had stood, where Palestrina had conducted, where Michelangelo had painted, and where even the Pope might hear our voices.

In June 2008, the Santa Barbara Choral Society was enjoying a two-week tour, scheduled for orchestra concerts in Rome, Florence, and Munich, with some a cappella concerts scattered in. Our tour manager took a long-shot chance and applied for the Society to sing in St. Peter's Basilica when we were in Rome; a rare privilege. Our local Catholic Bishop Thomas Curry, and another friend who had been a USA representative to the Vatican, wrote us letters of recommendation. Finally, we received the good news that we had been accepted for what turned out to be an historical moment in all of our singing careers.

We wound our way through the crowd in the immensity of the basilica, past the central Bernini Altar to the High Altar at the rear of the largest church in the world. Here the area was prepared for the Mass under a great, painted, arched ceiling. To one side was the organ console with a choir stall behind, where our chorus overflowed onto chairs. There was both reverential quiet in the space and a continuous bustle of functionaries coming and going, and tourists everywhere, in addition to the congregation who took their places in the pews in front of us. The Society members drank in the atmosphere and physically changed from hot, sweaty anxiety to cool excitement and awe.

The aura of history, drama, and holy presence vibrated in our minds. Kate and I looked at each other across the chorus and rolled our eyes. Neither of us could quite believe we were about to sing in St. Peter's. Two of our granddaughters, Samantha and Molly, were with the sopranos in the front. Sam was with a Catholic friend who was having the religious experience of her life, and Molly was staring straight up with her hand over her mouth. Our director, Jo Anne, spoke with the resident organist who had taken his place and she received permission to warm us up—quietly. She broke our spell of amazement and brought us down to earth with some softly sung scales that floated up into the rarified air, dispersing somewhere in space before reaching the ceiling.

The plan was to sing two motets, compositions on sacred texts, during the procession and three more during the distribution of communion. A cappella motets are my favorite music to sing, and we were well rehearsed and confident in our ethereal pieces. We would hear a pitch pipe and then be on our own without any accompaniment. Two pieces, "Sicut Cervus" and "Super Flumina Babylonis" were written by Giovanni Palestrina, who was music director at St. Peter's in 1551. His music has been sung there ever since, and was about to be performed again by our Society. The burden of centuries was in no way oppressive: it was inspirational. The other three pieces were "O Nata Lux de Lumine," the piece I sang for my Society audition, by Thomas Tallis; "Ubi Caritas," the one I sang to my cowboy friends, by Maurice Durufle; and lastly, "Vere Languores Nostros" by Tomas Victoria, a contemporary of Palestrina.

One of the mysteries of music is why one piece will be acceptable, but not special to one's hearing tastes, while another piece will spark a particular emotion and desire to hear or sing again.

The last piece we sang, by Victoria, always moves my emotions and inspires a desire to hear again equally worthy, but unable to ring that special inner bell. I love the piece and hope it is sung at my funeral, and also by me many more times before that event.

After our brief warm-up, we sat in silence while rows of pews filled with a few hundred worshipers, and the crowd of tourists hovered in the background. We each lived deep in our own thoughts; inspired, moved, and ready to sing. When we viewed the Vatican Mass celebrants forming their procession and moving into the public space, the organist turned and nodded to Jo Anne. She gave us her director's special face and hand signals that we knew so well. She told us, first, to settle down and focus; secondly, she signaled us to sing "north and south," not a flat tone, but a well-rounded note that would rise somewhere out of our innermost being, vertically projecting through the tops of our heads. That might sound peculiar, but after years of rehearsal we knew exactly what she meant. She gently raised her hands and we were off and soaring.

Voices on their own, a cappella, performing great music, are a celestial sensation in a huge cathedral. I know we all felt chills and heavy emotions as our notes gently billowed. I had a brief moment of listening to the music fill the space, but thrashed my concentration back to the bass music. Focus, Brooks, focus! I thought through the private prayer that I reserve for these moments: *Thank You, Lord, that You enable Your servant to sing for You;, and help me to do it well.*

When I sing in the chorus, I will never believe that an audience is actually hearing me; I am a small part of the music, and certainly always will be a modest contributor. Consequently, accolades are meaningless, even though we all like the occasional positive comment. But there is one honor I will always remember, and our Santa Barbara Choral Society should enshrine the moment in our history book. After the first motet, the somewhat terse and crusty-appearing elderly organist turned on his bench, gave us a smile, and gestured a thumbs-up approval!

As this was summer, we learned that the Pope was in his country palace, but we were graced with a cardinal who gave us a homily in Italian, which was lost to us travelers. A priest, with a splendid voice, led us through the sung Mass from the extensive altar. The responses were given by the congregation, but primarily led by three professional singers who stood just before us and sang into a microphone. When Communion was served we sang again, and this time more relaxed and concentrated; we had broken the nervous ice with our first motets during the procession.

The priests completed distributing communion before we had finished, and there was a touching moment when the officiant and his two assistants processed down from the High Altar and stood before us until we concluded, in order to administer to members of the choir who wanted to receive. Of course, we Episcopalians remained in our place, according to protocol, except for our two granddaughters who were swept up with their Catholic friends and joined the communicants. This was a breach of doctrine and Kate and I waited for the Swiss Guards to swing into action with their halberds. But charity prevailed, or at least nobody knew, and I am sure God was smiling.

The splendid moment was over all too soon, and we floated back through history, art, and architecture, and onto the buses. We extended our exhilarated mood with a splendid meal at an outdoor restaurant in the Piazza de Santa Maria Trastevre. A couple of young tenors had joined us with our granddaughters, as well as a few other special pals from the chorus. We were all in a state of euphoric shock. We needed the reassurance of returning to solid earth that only spaghetti and red wine could provide. The Italians, and the tourists who populated the neighboring piazza tables, were congenial company and celebrated the enthusiasm of our table that occasionally broke out in song with at least one happy birthday. We felt very much at home in Italy.

For a late-in life-couple who had no idea that our paths would ever take such a turn, Kate and I felt we had been to the mountain top. On our return home, one of my best post-trip moments was relating the experience to a devout Catholic pal who knew I was a solid Episcopalian, and both of us committed to our ways. When I finished relating the visit and explaining how I sang at a Mass in St. Peter's, he replied with astonishment, "You did what?"

* * *

A totally different experience awaited us at St. Paul's, London. In October 2011, the Royal Society of Church Music planned a special Evensong Service in St. Paul's Cathedral to celebrate the 150th anniversary of the *Hymns Ancient and Modern*. There are three great books endowed by the Anglican Church to the English-speaking Protestant world: the *King James Version* of the Bible, the *Book of Common Prayer* (source of Evensong), and the Hymns Ancient and Modern. The latter is the foundation for all subsequent church song books and was written 150 years ago, a compilation of all the known Anglican hymns that could be found.

The commemorative service would, of course, involve much singing by a volunteer chorus, and as we are RSCM members, Kate and I had signed on to join the choir. We were excited to sing in St. Paul's and planned our trip to England around the rehearsals and service.

Meanwhile, a few days before the service date, a protest movement in sympathy with the current "Occupy Wall Street" demonstrations initiated a camp site in the open space in front of St. Paul's. The crowd and tents had been thrown out of a square in front of the English equivalent of Wall Street and settled instead on the more neutral site in front of St. Paul's. Two-hundred or so tents and activists lapped against the Cathedral steps like a tide moving on shoreline rocks, depositing the flotsam of the world.

The source of the protesters' angst appeared to be capitalism in general and bankers in particular. Of course, this had nothing to do with St. Paul's, an innocent neighbor to the publicity-driven settlement. Even though the public soon became bored by the movement's lack of content, message, or alternative positive policy in any coherent form, the street people began to receive wide publicity as their numbers and photogenic tent site prospered.

On the first day of occupation, a well-meaning Cathedral priest had welcomed the demonstrators in the name of free speech and received wide review on television. He had not considered the potential hazard if the protest turned ugly because of anarchists, looters, and other criminal elements, as sometimes happens. In two days the Cathedral crypt store and restaurant were closed, and in five days St. Paul's overreacted and shut its doors completely. The Cathedral dean issued a statement suggesting that the protesters had received their publicity, and it was now time to move on. As this implied that St. Paul's might be a party to police action, the first welcoming priest resigned from the Cathedral staff.

A few days later the Cathedral opened its doors, and shortly thereafter the dean, also surprisingly, resigned his position. The entire Cathedral response seemed a pointless overreaction. Kate and I followed the developing drama closely because of the upcoming service and attended an Evensong service during the occupation and before the closure. There was little noise from the protesters, and we saw no discernable problem for the Cathedral. Kate remarked that the tents resembled a colony of burrowing animals leaving multicolored surface humps from their underground excavations.

I was among the first inside the Cathedral, when the great doors opened again, to attend the noon service marking the reopening of the Cathedral. Once more, I saw no problem between the protesters and St. Paul's. The clergy dithered and the protesters stayed put.

Unfortunately, the shutdown coincided with our service and opportunity to sing, and the RSCM was forced to move their venue to Southwark Cathedral, across the Thames but not far from St. Paul's. The Southwark Cathedral has a venerable history beginning in Roman times, punctuated by fires, disrepair, encroaching roads and railroads, and operates more as a large parish church than as a cathedral. It is a vital institution today, but as the world's churches go, something of a poor relation to the famous St. Paul's. True to their energy and generosity, and with rapid adjustments, they accommodated the large RSCM service.

At 2:00 p.m. prior to the 5:00 service, the hundred-and-fifty or so members of the volunteer choir filled about half of the nave for rehearsal. We divided into sections, and the thirty or so basses sat shoulder-to-shoulder in a friendly block of pews, curious as to how the rehearsal would go. Because of a misplaced confidence in my sight-reading abilities and confusion about whether the service would actually take place, I confess that I had put in less than my usual preparation and practice. This would lead to embarrassing consequences later.

Our first piece was a dramatic choral fanfare, including some tricky passages and rhythms, that brought the choir to a standstill in the first run-through; always a bad sign. We never did get it quite right, despite the competent and optimistic leadership of Matthew Owens, choirmaster of Wells Cathedral. My years of choral singing, and my improvement along the way, mistakenly led me to believe that I could sing out with minimal rehearsal. In my defense, I believed the music was easier than it actually turned out to be; I should have been more prepared.

The Southwark Cathedral filled to capacity for the service, with the excitement of a meaningful occasion unaffected by the change in venue. The dignity and drama of the celebration was as good as the English know how to do, and the ceremony proceeded with elegance. The splendid, colorful procession of clergy and dignitaries formed, and began to process as we launched into our choral fanfare.

The music sounded very much better than it did in rehearsal, and I joined in with a will. Toward the middle of the piece there was a full-out, double forte phrase, ending with three half notes singing, "Praise! Praise! Praise!" In the excitement of the moment I sang out and realized that my own third "Praise!" decisively and firmly landed when 149 other singers were on their second "Praise!" My three for two solo confused and frustrated my neighbors, but there is never a moment in singing when one can grovel or apologize. The ancient Cathedral was full of important tombs, and if one had been empty, I would gladly have crawled in.

The remaining program was mostly hymns, and one melodic anthem led by a soprano with a generous and clear voice echoing beautifully into the high ceiling. Another short piece was an original composition written for the occasion and sung with gusto. Needless to say, my remaining contributions were subdued and unremarkable. Everyone felt pleased with the service except me; I only wanted to apologize to the world for my singing blunder.

As of this writing in early 2012, the world's "occupy" campsites have mostly been shut down, either by negotiation or by force. But the campers in front of St. Paul's, facing a winter of cold discontent, remained more or less in place until late February. St. Paul's, at one time, offered to erect a symbolic tent in the Cathedral, demonstrating sympathy with the rights of the campers, if the rest would go away. The clergy, less one canon and one dean, also offered to engage in some kind of dialogue with the protesters, although the specifics of their demands have been vague. The protesters and Cathedral ran on parallel tracks without convergence until, finally, the campers exhausted their righteous indignation, the London authorities ran out of patience, and the courts depleted their anarchical indulgence. Visitors now cross the abandoned steam-cleaned square to visit St. Paul's in the traditional London atmosphere of welcome and tranquility. Kate and I are still somewhat grumpy about our missed opportunity to sing in the historic and venerable St. Paul's, and hope the future will bring this about in a less confrontational world.

Chapter Eighteen

$\mathcal{P}$ARTY $\mathcal{T}$IME

● ● ●

MY CAREER AS A VINTNER led me into a number
of wine societies, including the venerable Chevaliers du Tastevin,
a worldwide organization that celebrates the splendid wines of
Burgundy. This group is famous for sumptuous dinners with great
wine and entertainment. The Los Angeles chapter decided, in
2009, to hold their annual white-tie gala at the posh Santa Barbara
Biltmore Hotel. As I was a local member, the Chevalier officers
put me on the dinner committee and then, for my sins, appointed
me entertainment chair for the evening.

Many years before, I had performed that function for the same
annual dinner held at the Los Angeles Beverly Wilshire Hotel.
For that ambitious affair, I hired opera performers to sing an aria
between each course to add the charm of music and enhance the
menu description of the exotic dishes being served. The food and

wine were to be described by the master of ceremonies for the evening, the famous radio and television personality, Art Linkletter. Before serving each course a short description explained the relationship of the food and wine as reflected in the musical piece. For example, he introduced the main course in this way: "The next course will be a fillet steak with a rich Beaujolais sauce accompanied by a Chambertin Clos de Beze 1971. This fare is reminiscent of the bull-ring drama and the famous 'Toreador' song from Bizet's opera, *Carmen*"! While the food was being served, a baritone sang the lusty aria, and the dinner guests were charmed and amazed.

For the last course, a Viennese chocolate torte was served with a Firestone Late Harvest Riesling. The Burgundy society used our wine because no dessert wine is made in the Burgundy area, and also because I was on the dinner committee. That course was described as being reminiscent of a scene from the Strauss opera *Die Fledermaus*. As this was the finale, we had all four singers belt out the famous waltz chorus and, in addition, Kate had choreographed a mini ballet with four Santa Barbara ballet dancers. The quartet of beautiful young girls charmed the audience, first, on the stage with the singers, and then, dancing through the tables as the opera stars sang the lively waltz. Chevalier members who attended that dinner still claim there were at least two dozen ballerinas who leaped over the tables. Opera and Art Linkletter, with ballerinas thrown in, provided amazing dinner entertainment!

At the more recent Santa Barbara occasion, the dinner committee agreed, after much discussion, with my recommendation to adopt a musical theme again, and of course the Santa Barbara Choral Society was chosen. It did not take much persuasion to inspire the chorus to join the party with song, and they were very much up for the gig. The ballroom at the Biltmore could easily accommodate one-hundred-and-fifty Chevalier diners, so we arranged the tables to leave room for our ninety singers, with the conductor's podium and the grand piano at one end of the elegant ballroom. The entertainment for the evening was never announced, so the Chevaliers could only speculate about what the strange arrangement indicated and what was to come.

After the first course, the dinner chair rose to the microphone and said, "Ladies and gentlemen, please welcome the Santa Barbara Choral Society." Whereupon, ninety singers filed into the room and Jo Anne Wasserman took her place on the podium. Conversation ceased as chorus and diners silently faced off across the room. Perhaps it was the refreshments at the separate singers' party or the enthusiasm of the grand evening, but the music took off with an explosion. The piece we had chosen was the third movement from Mozart's *Requiem* beginning with, "*Dies irae. Dies illa!*" translated from Latin, " Day of rage. Day of trouble!" With high notes and double forte directions we were given a license to sing out, and we lifted the ballroom roof with a torrent of sound. The formal diners probably expected some gentle French motet or entertaining show tune, but what they got was full-out Mozart. One could hear silver forks hitting the plates and see jaws dropping as the fast and furious piece came to a sudden conclusion. The singers trooped out as the stunned guests wondered aloud, "Who are those people?" And they wanted more.

Between the next two courses the Society marched in again, but this time sang something more traditional, "If Music be the Food of Love, Sing on." The volume was more tempered and romantic, and the diners were equally pleased and less overwhelmed. The chorus retreated to their own party room, knowing that they had a success going from the enthusiastic applause.

The stately Chevalier du Tastevin Society attempts to sing a song something like a children's playtime song as their worldwide signature tune, which does not need to be translated. If any wine particularly pleases, or if any other need arises to show approbation, someone will stand, raise their hands, palms forward and fingers spread, and do a rotating wave while singing, "La-la, la-la, la-la-la-la-la-la" and then, while clapping to the rhythm, repeat, "La-la-la, la-la-la, la-la-la." It is basic music that most members can manage, even during a long evening and a lot of wine. The idea sounds juvenile but, with spirit, the simple piece adds to the occasion.

As we trooped in the third time, we had a well-rehearsed gag up our sleeves. The dinner chair rose to the mike and introduced me to lead a special arrangement of the traditional "La-la." The Chavaliers expected the usual traditional song, when I raised my white-gloved hands and nodded to our conductor, Jo Anne Wasserman, who waved the downbeat to the chorus. What came out was a soprano singing an aria from *La Traviata* except using the "la-la" words. I lowered my hands and shook my head at our conductor who looked puzzled. She shrugged and again gave the downbeat, but this time all the men sang the chorus of the "Volga Boatman," again with "la-las." I stamped my foot and waved them off again. But this time, on the downbeat, a baritone "la-la'd" part of Beethoven's *Ninth Symphony*. Once again, and this time, all the women "la'd" a chorus from Puccini's *Madam Butterfly* until I could stop them, waving my arms and grimacing with frustration. I shook my head and Jo Anne shrugged and mimicked, "If not this, then what?" I gestured and mouthed, "One more time, and let's get it right!" On this downbeat, the chorus belted out a four-part original rendition of the traditional, but never as elegantly presented, "la-la," and this time the guests did their best to join in. The diners were delighted and amused that we finally got it right. Guests and chorus had a splendid evening and once more demonstrated what singing can do for a party.

Our success of that evening was endorsed at the Chevalier

annual dinner held the following year. The entertainment chair for that grand affair was a director of the venerable Los Angeles Master Chorale made up of professional singers and one of the premier choral organizations in the world. Thirty members of the Chorale entertained the diners with beautiful and elegant French songs, brilliantly presented, and very much in keeping with the Chevaliers' heritage. Those of us from Santa Barbara admitted the excellence of the entertainment, but could not imagine that they had as much fun as we enjoyed at *our* dinner.

* * *

A much less formal occasion was planned for my sixty-fifth birthday party, when I was just beginning my singing career. We had invited a couple of hundred people for the celebration in a large hay barn and everyone arrived in elegant Western garb in the mood for a party. The guests were seated, enjoying a western buffet and buckets of local wine, and Kate and I were happy together surrounded by family and best pals.

Then, on cue, two opera singers stepped to the stage to sing the emotional finale from Leonard Bernstein's opera, *Candide*: "You've been a fool and so have I, but come and be my wife, and let us strive before we die to make some sense of life." At that moment, about two dozen of our friends and family who could sing, including some who had professional voices, stood up at their tables joining Kate and me. All of us gradually made our way through the tables to the stage while belting out the chorus: "We're neither pure nor wise nor good, we'll do the best we know. We'll build our house and chop our wood, and make our garden grow. And make our garden grow...!" When we finished there was not a dry eye in the barn. Just then the birthday cakes came in and we took the roof off the barn with the good old "Happy Birthday," and I took the liberty of singing at my own party. Later, two of my pals wearing gorilla suits ran into the party and kidnapped Kate, but that is a different story.

* * *

The same large barn also served on another occasion as the venue for a rare evening of serious singing. Opera Santa Barbara is a local organization that stages full and glorious productions, mostly in the Granada Theater. Through the years they have presented some impressive classic operas, but this particular summer they decided to do something different for a fundraiser. *La Fanciulla del West*, the "Girl of the Golden West," is a dramatic opera by Giacomo Puccini, which may never have been produced quite like the show planned in our barn. The idea was to have three first-class international opera stars carry the drama on a small stage, while I narrated to make up the parts of story that could not be portrayed without a full cast and set.

To fill in the lack of a full production, we devised a men's chorus to act as background western characters and sing the songs "Shenandoah" in the first act, and "Streets of Laredo" in the second act. Some of the singers, like the chair of the fundraising committee and me, were known to the audience, and we had a moment of murmuring before we convinced them that we were a serious part of the opera. While the unorthodox songs might have fallen short of the opera stars in quality, our music fit the story and our enthusiasm was not to be denied. Additionally, one side of the barn was open to a large grass pasture, and we dragooned four local cowboy pals to gallop their horses back and forth to act out the chase scene and then bring the villain of the plot in to justice. The bad guy was also an important tenor who had a serious problem with having a noose put around his precious vocal-cord neck and dallied to a saddle horn!

On that evening, two-hundred-and-fifty, high-rolling Santa Barbarans showed up in all manner of amazing western outfits and sat at tables for the show. We broke in the middle of the opera for a long interval, including a barbecue and local wine. Everything worked with unique style: the opera conductor, who also played the piano; the opera stars, who eventually figured out that they were supposed to have fun; the local men's chorus, who were convincing; the narration that filled in the gaps with western color; and the mounted cowboys playing their part like veterans. It even rained on the tin barn roof during part of the opera. The last moment of the libretto has the hero and girl walking off with a dramatic duet. Instead of off-stage, we had them walking off onto a pasture through oak trees singing their finale. The audience was in the spirit, fully enjoyed the show, and even gathered around the piano to serenade themselves after the opera.

* * *

My favorite party-like moment took place during a Christmas concert the Choral Society had arranged in our Firestone/Walker Brewery warehouse, which also stores wine cases and barrels. The open warehouse seated a large audience, and, as it was lined with empty wooden wine barrels and had a metal roof, offered amazingly good acoustics. The opening two pieces were quiet, serious, and emotionally beautiful motets, both "Ave Marias." Before the second, our conductor, Jo Anne Wasserman, hesitated until the large space was completely still and silent, then raised her arms to bring the chorus quietly into the music. At that precise moment, behind some stacked wine barrels where a reception was being prepared, a wine cork was popped from the bottle and could be heard clearly in the silence by everyone in the warehouse.

With that tiny but total disruption, Jo Anne's facial expressions contorted in nanoseconds from irritation, to questioning, to resignation, to acceptance; then she dropped her arms and began laughing. With that, our eighty-member chorus and three-hundred-and-fifty-member audience exploded into laughter, and it was some minutes before we could regain our composure and begin the piece again. The moment was a classic expression of being in the Santa Ynez Valley, where wine is a way of life, and beautiful music is appreciated with joy.

Choral singers do not need to be arrayed in white-tie outfits behind a symphony orchestra, or wearing horned helmets on the opera stage; they can be anywhere their imagination can take them. Kate and I have also learned that the performers can often have more fun than the audience.

Chapter Nineteen

Good Impressions

● ● ●

SINGING IS UNIVERSAL and this leads to many interesting events and exchanges. A singing experience, either with foreigners visiting the States or a group of Americans going overseas, can lead to a positive lasting impression and enhanced relationships, possibly better than the United Nations could ever accomplish.

A fellow member of the Choral Society once asked if a touring group he was helping to organize, called "The King's Chapel Singers," hailing from Gibraltar, could visit our winery on their tour when they drove through the Santa Ynez Valley from Monterey to Ventura. I replied I would be delighted to host them, but as choruses like to sing, why not visit our St. Mark's on the way and either hold a concert or, better yet, an Evensong with our congregation. He agreed, and the game was on.

The Gibraltar group took their name from one of the oldest church locations in history, at the crossroads of the world. Who knows what ancient, pre-Christian rituals were performed at this venerable site? Evolving mankind has lived in Gibraltar's caves since the dawn of time, and in ancient recorded history the famous rock has housed Phoenicians, Carthaginians, Romans, and Visigoths. Some time around the AD 400s the Goths built a Christian chapel, and that was the foundation for the later King's Chapel.

Muslim Moors and local Christians celebrated their faiths at the chapel site until, finally, in 1462, the Franciscans established Christianity for the Spanish. In 1704, the British became permanent owners of the famous turf that includes a massive rock mountain and, with the English, the Anglican Church has prevailed up to the present. Californians are amazed by such an historic pedigree, and our local St. Mark's warmed to the prospect of hosting singers associated with such an illustrious past. Of course, our St. Mark's church was built in the town of Los Olivos only in the 1980s.

Our enthusiasm was somewhat muted on hearing that this group was not the Chapel choir, but rather a chorus that rehearsed in the famous chapel and adopted the King's Chapel name. We then discovered that they did not know the Evensong service, which we had imagined would be second nature to their old-world Anglican heritage. But our welcome mat had been put out, and we were eager to learn what these new friends from Gibraltar would bring.

Their busy schedule was set for them to arrive on a Monday afternoon, rehearse in the church, bus to the winery for a tour and wine tasting, return to St. Mark's for a concert, then to the Firestone/Walker Brewery restaurant for a pizza dinner. Finally, they would be taken to various parish members' homes for the night. The group of about two dozen singers proved, on arrival, to be a unique mixture of English, Spanish, Mediterranean, and North African extraction, and the most pleasant people in the world.

We had set up our church and advertised the concert locally for a late Sunday afternoon concert. The chorus presented a mixed program of Anglican, African, and contemporary songs, and additionally a solo from their very talented accompanying concert pianist. The Chapel Singers performed with energy and joy in their red blazer outfits and were received enthusiastically by the somewhat sparse audience, mostly made up of church friends. The last three pieces were sung with our St. Mark's choir joining together with theirs. The most memorable piece was a song written by Eric Clapton after the death of his son titled, "Tears in Heaven." It was beautiful and moving, and we sang as though our two choirs were one. Their director was enthusiastic and outgoing, and we easily filtered in among their singers. We were separated by nationality, history, distance, and heritage, but we were absolutely, and most warmly, united in music.

The pleasures of pizza, local wine, and beer united us further at the Firestone/Walker Brewery restaurant. I noticed that our locals and the Gibraltarians were completely mixed and interspersed at the long tables, engaging in animated exchanges. They had presented me with a Gibraltar flag and I seized the moment to hold it up and ask if a song went with it. Of course, they all stood and rendered a beautiful and hearty national anthem which was new and incomprehensible to us Americans. This inspired the locals to reply with a four- part "America the Beautiful," worthy of any beer hall.

The group dispersed to the homes of their Santa Ynez Valley hosts, to meet again next morning, full of local Danish pastry, for their trip south. We locals agreed that it had been a most pleasant and interesting visit as we waved them down the road. The tradition of exchanging singing groups and chorales internationally is a force for holding the world together. Of course, local beer and pizza help also.

* * *

Just as local musical efforts serve our communities, they also serve to define, to visitors, who we are as a country. A visitor can learn much from observing the music of a country. Our granddaughter, Samantha, who is also a singer, gained an increased affection for Australia when she chanced on an Evensong service in Sydney.

In 2010, twenty-two-year-old Samantha decided to have a traveling adventure after graduating from Bowdoin College. She had sung choir solos from time to time, joined an a cappella group in college, and traveled with the Choral Society trip to Italy, so she was familiar with choral singing and choirs. She had heard about my book project, so when she stumbled on an Evensong service at St. James Anglican Church during her travels through Sydney, she decided to wander in. Here is Samantha's spontaneous impressions of the occasion, partly penned while sitting in the pew, and immediately thereafter.

"Lit by colored night lights, St. James stood next to the Supreme Court of New South Wales on King Street, steps north of the luxurious and surprisingly green Hyde Park of Sydney. A young girl touring solo through the magnificent city decides to stop at the oldest surviving church, with a tanned stone and brick exterior blending with the neighboring buildings.

"The sounds that escape the door let the young wanderer know that this place has more to offer. Sure enough, she reads signs around the building to learn that this is a holy place, a place of calm and serenity amidst the chaos of a booming and exciting city.

"The vibrant sounds lure the young lass in. A Priest in white robes greets her with a smile inside the towering wood door and asks her if she would like a program. A choir is rehearsing for Evensong and he tells her the service will start in twenty minutes. As she peers into the beautiful and brightly lit church, the sound of the singers fills her with warmth and light. The decision of whether to continue on her tourist track or settle for a few minutes is not a difficult one. Although she has spent her day searching through the city for a new wallet and proper pair of walking shoes, and scouring through all the touristy venues, this young lady wants a few moments to breathe, sing and perhaps shed a nostalgic tear before she continues on and joins some of her friends for a posh inner city dinner.

"The rehearsal has finished now, and while inhaling the familiar smells of the wood pews, old hymnals, and candles, this girl's emotions stir. She has a few moments of silence to breathe in the atmosphere she knows from childhood Sunday school and children's choir rehearsals at St. Mark's in the Valley back in California. Time stands still for her, and if she closes her eyes it feels that nothing moves around her but memories of baptisms, Christmas caroling, flowery decorations, a funeral in the chapel, singing Handel's *Messiah* around the altar, and, of course, as much cake as possible at the coffee hour after the service.

"The organ starts on a low, soft and slow theme as people fill in. An elderly couple, he in a wool check suit jacket and burgundy tie and she with a beige trench coat and colorful scarf, sit at the other end of the pew and give her a smile. She is delighted that she will have neighbors to share the service who seem so warm and caring. Everyone stands as the choir and clergy enter the church. As the organ's chords rise and fall in familiar if lugubrious melody, the young lady surveys the church to see the surrounding paintings, inscriptions, stained glass, and flower arrangements. The most impressive sight is forward, behind the altar and choir at the very back wall: a gold covered semi-dome behind the cross. The gold wall gleams in the lights, and glows in regal magnificence.

"The young girl's head turns to the direction of the voices that now sing the opening prayers. The eight sung call and response lines enrapture her. The Priest sings in an aged and worn voice, barely clinging to the notes. The single Soprano leads her fellows in the soft but powerful response, and their melodies fall into place one after the other with harmonious ringing. Her voice is pure, clear, and truly angelic as the choir opens with four part harmony and the church fills with the traditional and comforting music.

"Throughout the service the young girl is on the brink of tears. She does not pay much attention to the words of the readings or songs, but instead focuses on the melody and sound of their voices. They come alive with color, even in the minor, haunting keys. The gold of the semi-dome is echoed in the light of the Soprano's voice, and the young girl breathes in the sounds and colors, enjoying every second of this beautiful peace."

Such is the mood and atmosphere of Evensong. The meaning of that visit is the warm and reassuring thought that both the service and the welcome are alive and well in that faraway, late afternoon. My granddaughter's story inspires me to travel to Sydney someday to thank the priest and St. James for being there for Samantha, and reminds me again of the positive force of music in international relations.

* * *

Another year, Kate and I attended a Sunday morning service at St. Andrew's Anglican Church on the Caribbean island of Antigua. The large church was overfull because the central Cathedral of St. John's was closed for repairs, and the St. Andrew's parish temporarily served both congregations. We were given a strong and friendly welcome to the church and felt very much at home.

The Communion Service emphasized community alongside the familiar liturgy, complete with a resounding "happy birthday" for that week's honorees. Cold-comfort English churches can only dream and long for the Caribbean climate and island breezes that wafted through the church. The choir music was lively and enthusiastic, along traditional Anglican hymn form, and lacked some choral finesse but abounded in enthusiasm and was strongly joined by the congregation. We loved our moment with Antiguan Anglicans and wondered why more tourists don't choose to get off the tour busses and worship with the welcoming locals.

Chapter Twenty

ROAD TRIP

• • •

THE PERSON WHO coined the phrase, "Getting there is half the fun," never experienced the questionable joys of organizing an international choral excursion. In the end, the Santa Barbara Choral Society enjoyed a successful and memorable summer 2011 trip to Spain, but the early stages presented frustrating challenges.

As good organizations will do, we solicited our membership well ahead of time to assess interest in a three-to-four-thousand dollar, two-week trip, and Spain came out as the overwhelming country of choice. On the strength of that survey, the tour committee spent many hours with our travel company, ACFEA Tour Consultants, meticulously planning the two-week concert tour through Spain. Later, at sign-up and deposit time, the realities of a continuing recession and other personal problems resulted in commitments from our Society members well under the necessary numbers for the group rates and a workable chorus. We engaged in fundraising for financial help for some of our singers, but that effort came up short as well.

Faced with the possibility of canceling altogether, which meant suffering the loss of early deposits our organization could ill afford, the Society Board decided to open the trip to groups and singers outside our members. We publicized that openings in our trip were for qualified singers, recommended to our music director by their organization's director, and otherwise capable of performing the works we had planned. This brought an immediate and enthusiastic response. Choral travelers from the University of California Alumni Chorus and singers from Sonoma, British Columbia, and Hawaii sent in their applications and deposits. Our numbers swelled with new friends-to-be and we soon made up the necessary number of travelers; but, of course, we wondered how we would all get along and what would be the resulting quality of music. We planned two programs, Gabriel Faure's *Requiem* with local orchestras, and an a cappella program that included a range from classical motets to modern spirituals.

Our final travelers totaled ninety-four, including sixty-eight singers, thirty-eight from the Santa Barbara Choral Society, and thirty from other groups. We numbered twenty-three sopranos, twenty-two altos, nine tenors and fourteen basses. With this mix, we balanced in sections and voices, but could not predict quality and blending. The music scores were sent to everyone with the expectation that all would arrive well rehearsed and, hopefully, had even memorized four pieces. We had chosen black concert dresses for the women and, after much soul-searching about whether the men should wear formal jackets, the committee decided on light-weight black shirts to wear in the expected heat.

Our full Society chorus had rehearsed together extensively,

and had, twice, performed the Faure Requiem in Santa Barbara; but the unrehearsed newcomers were taken on faith. Finally the departure date arrived and the group landed in Madrid on a Saturday evening. The moment of truth would come the next day at 8:00 a.m., jet lag or no, with our first rehearsal in a basement meeting room of our hotel.

Our music director, Jo Anne Wasserman, convened her unknown chorus into a rough circle in the cramped basement room. We shook hands with our new neighbors, ready to sing in the confined space. An advantage for a well-rehearsed chorus is that the musical director has the ability to place and rearrange the singers. Certain voices complement one another while some combinations exacerbate problems. Of course, Jo Anne never had time or opportunity to match voices, with so many of our singers being total strangers to her, but she had the responsibility of performing a concert the next day and was prepared to do what she could do in her short rehearsal.

Jo Anne is a baseball fan who avidly supports the Los Angeles Dodgers. She knows that successful ball teams first emphasize the basics; running, throwing, hitting, and catching win games. The finer points of tactics, batting order, double plays, and other products of sophisticated baseball are important, but the basics come first in training. Accordingly, she began our basement session with simple scales to work our voices together, then worked, in the time allotted, through all our pieces to be performed that trip, stressing basic rhythms and wording, ignoring the subtleties of tone, pronunciation, volume, and other fine points of choral singing that produce a memorable concert. She discovered that the basics were fairly secure with our newly merged chorus and that the newcomers had done their homework; she had a chorus. During the trip she would work on tuning. By the time she began thinking about details, our rehearsal was over, and we moved out to the bus that was scheduled to take us for a tour of the ancient fortress city of Toledo.

On arriving at Toledo most of us made a beeline for the Cathedral where we toured, in awe, of the space, history, and art that abounded. The huge building was designed for music and we were all born to sing and inspired to add our music to the centuries of sacred song that had filled the space. We soon won over a friendly, but slightly skeptical, cleric in charge who ushered us into a side chapel to perform two of our pieces extemporaneously.

Jo Anne had urged us to memorize four of the pieces for just such an occasion, but many of our group, even the Society members, had fallen short in that expectation. The two motets written in four-part harmony, Viadana's "Exsultate Justi" and Palestrina's "Sicut Cervus," were something well beyond basic a cappella campfire songs, and if the sections drifted apart, there were not many reorganization points in the difficult score. But Cathedrals were made for miracles.

Kate and I, and some others, had brought along the music scores, just in case, and we formed little huddles of singers looking over shoulders as Jo Anne bravely led us into the works. In that amazing space, and with the professional voices leading the rest of us, we sounded warm and spiritual, but there were obvious mistakes that should have warned us about our lack of experience in working together. The beaming cleric and gathered tourists thanked us for the musical moment, and our new choral group took delight and optimistic, if unwarranted, confidence in our ability to carry off the next day's challenge.

The first concert the next day was our piano and a cappella program in a large Madrid church. Mark Sumner, the music director of the UC Alumni Chorus as well as other choruses in the San Francisco Bay area, joined us as pianist and soloist and was a hero of the tour. Not only was he very competent in his work, he also modestly matched and enhanced Jo Anne's direction and encouraged our entire chorus. He took his place at the piano and we all took our positions in our new surroundings around the altar area of the church for a long rehearsal before the concert. Our first efforts seemed to go well enough but were still tentative. We all gazed at the architecture, paintings, tapestries, statues, and metalwork and realized the privilege we were enjoying to sing in this amazing Spanish venue, and knew we must be worthy.

At performance time, the church was packed with several hundred locals eager to hear what America had brought to their parish. We all were accustomed to extensive preparation and perhaps did not fully realize that our travel time lag and lack of experience together might take its toll. A humiliating choral moment that many, including Kate and me, had never imagined could happen, did happen. Twice. Once, the result of a wrong pitch pipe note in Victoria's "Ave Maria" and, again, with a hesitant tenor section at the beginning of Dawson's "There is a Balm in Gilead." Jo Anne brought us to a complete halt and made us begin again. She remained poised and in charge and our restarts worked perfectly, but the moments of individual trauma brought us a new focus for the rest of the tour.

Our lack of rehearsal time and unfamiliarity with one another, as well as the unknown orchestras, could potentially take our musical train off the tracks, and some of us felt we occasionally approached derailment again. But from that first concert on, we held ourselves together and never had a noticeable mishap. In that first concert, only Jo Anne's presence and calm demeanor had kept us on course and prevented the stops and restarts from spreading panic or shattering confidence. But even with those two problem moments, the audience loved us and we performed our encores after a standing ovation in the packed church. Afterwards, one man came up to me, obviously very moved. He had lived in Washington D. C. for twelve years and loved America. "You have brought the best of America!" he exclaimed. "Thank you for bringing your country here!"

Our next stop, the town of Cuenca, gave us the opportunity to perform Gabriel Faure's *Requiem* with the Orchestra Filarmonica de Cuenca in the beautiful Cathedral of Our Lady of Grace, set in the historic hill-town square. Our high altar space was somewhat cramped and featured a decorative grill surrounding the entire orchestra and chorus space. Jo Anne sensed that we were somehow singing only to that space, so she made us focus our voices to the back window, throwing our arms out to the back wall of the church to stimulate our projection. Her gimmick made an appreciable difference.

The best standing space I could find was at the back of the high altar, which moved me from the basses and baritones in front of the altar, but turned out to be the perfect spot when Mark Sumner and Jeff Warlick, splendid basses and true musicians, came to stand on either side of me. Good company makes choral singing worthwhile, particularly to a relative newcomer, and I had the best for this concert. We all live for hints of approbation, and one of those rare moments came when Jeff told me—and I believe he meant it—that he enjoyed singing with me. The musical ego of a late-life singer, such as I, is as fragile as my pitch, and such words of encouragement bring an all-important confidence as well as a warm glow.

Some of us were more aware than others of the concerns felt by local parish and clergy in receiving a crowd of American singers of unknown religious backgrounds into their church. We would arrive and store our packs in the pews and then, usually, search for the bathrooms, leaving noise and confusion in our wake. However, the locals were understanding and welcoming, as long as we more or less behaved. It was necessary to show respect to the altar, particularly keeping music folders and water bottles off the sacred space. Those of us who were aware, finally resorted to stealing the bottles from the less thoughtful, and hiding them at the back of the church. The audience always demonstrated inspiring friendliness and enthusiasm to welcome us.

Working with a new and totally unfamiliar orchestra presents a formidable challenge to a conductor, especially when there is a short time to rehearse the instruments before worrying about adding the chorus to the mix. In a matter of minutes, Jo Anne had to assess the musicians she would be working with, as well as the unique acoustics of the Cathedral space, meanwhile asserting her authority and gaining confidence and respect. Here in our Spanish church venue, a new mix of singers, an unfamiliar orchestra in a cramped, caged space, and only two hours of rehearsal before performing to an unknown audience, was a moment of truth for our director. There were crucial decisions to be made about which problems to attack, and which errors to let slide, because she could not do more than was possible, given the circumstances.

In the evening event, the Cathedral was again packed with a few hundred locals, and our concert came off beautifully with no obvious errors and we received a standing ovation again. Given all the factors, it seemed like a miracle, and we were quite satisfied with ourselves.

We all celebrated with a late, for us, but normal for the Spanish, celebration dinner in a large restaurant on the river below the town. The occasion was billed as a communal birthday party for the five or six of us whose birthdays fell during the tour. The series of "Happy Birthday" songs grew in volume and harmony, and came to include waiters and cooks before the night was out. I had an emotional moment in toasting the occasion and it went something like this: "Ladies and gentlemen, I would like to celebrate our concert that began at 8:30 and my tour which began fifteen minutes later at 8:45 tonight. At that moment, I came to know that, as a chorus, we make very good music, we're representing our art well, we're representing our country well, and we're all having a splendid experience doing this. So here's to a great concert tour!" The crowd knew I was right on and the words brought a great cheer. The food and wine were perfect and lavish, and the birthdays' party continued into the night. I realized, if I ever had any doubt, that the age of seventy-five was turning out to be all right.

The next day a group of us were recovering at a late lunch, and the topic of audience appreciation and applause came up. My pal, Bob Lally, mentioned that he loves ovations, particularly if the audience is moved to stand while applauding. I replied that I do not really pay attention to applause and, in fact, never believe the audience is recognizing me, but rather people like Bob, or Kate, or especially Jo Anne. I went on to say, "I'm amazed to hear applause. In fact, I'm amazed that I'm on the stage singing at all." Then Jo Anne had to pipe up and say, "I'm amazed you're here too, Brooks!" Ah, well, such is the life of an honest wannabe bass, but I felt good that our director could take me apart in good humor.

Our major work, the Faure Requiem, is in Latin and some of our other works are in Spanish, but most in English. Our audiences were all Spanish and, in trying to communicate in our limited "Spanglish" with them after concerts, we realized that very few spoke English. However, the language never mattered, as music is universal and overcomes language, culture, or any other barriers.

Another pleasant aspect of choral music is a complete generational indifference. We had the extraordinary pleasure of singing on the tour with our daughter and two granddaughters in complete equality of effort, with no consideration of age. We were committed to performing the music as people and voices on the most fundamentally level basis. Very satisfying and refreshing and a cause for loving equality when Granddad is just another bass voice.

The tour continued with adventures and song until our last stop, Barcelona; Kate and I fell in love with the city. We were unprepared for the uniqueness, imagination, and excitement of the town. We can only suggest that Barcelona must be visited. It should not be missed. The city has spaciousness, made for evening walks, and a decorative individuality to homes and apartment buildings that indicate hospitality and artistic vision.

The world famous Cathedral La Sagrada Familia, designed in the late 1800s by the seminal architect, Antoni Gaudi, moved me as much as any work of art in my experience. The unfinished Cathedral can only be described as an explosion of imagination, and walking through the extraordinary building is a mind-expanding experience. My deeply suspicious view of modern art appreciably shifted with the realization that there is creativity of great worth and inspiration yet to be realized in this world. Gaudi's potent vision hit me between the eyes when I entered the amazing building. Here was a human statement of great proportion and sanctity in a myriad of dimensions. And better yet, Gaudi was a choral singer, as well as architectural genius, which perhaps explained the generous choir space that could accommodate a thousand singers.

Equally impactful, although on a smaller scale, is the Palau de la Musica Catalana, the palace of music. The theater building defies description as there is so much artistic action teeming. The guidebook tells of "a dreaming palace of wonders," and a "hall of light and sound," and a "magical fishbowl." It is all that and more, and defies description except to say that it must be seen by anyone who appreciates music or original thought. Architectural lines, columns, glass, sculptures, ceramics, tiles, paintings, arches, balustrades, mosaics, and more, provide an inspirational surrounding beyond any performance hall we had ever experienced. The artistic media present a profusion of varied flower themes, turning the space into an architectural garden.

To walk into the building is to enter a magic, musical kingdom. Performers can be only at their best in a setting that provides such comfortable two-thousand- audience seats and brilliant acoustics.

Guided tours of about forty are first introduced by a short film presenting the history of the Palau. Our group included Jo Anne and some of our best voices, and there was an electrical current running through the group when we were ushered into the main hall. We were singers, and the venerable tradition of performances from the beautiful stage beckoned for one more offering, spontaneous and heartfelt, from us. Additionally, we all had our music scores with us in preparation for a later rehearsal. Our guide was a unique and generous soul. When asked if we could sing, at first he wanted to check with security, but then he looked at our faces and said, "Well, five minutes, and please take care." We assembled on the stage in an instant with our music sheets at the ready.

Jo Anne chose Tomas Victoria's "Ave Maria" and Palestrina's "Sicut Cervus." The motets poured out of our throats and souls into that splendid space. We sang, as they say, better than we were able, realizing that we were enjoying the experience of a lifetime. Our music mingled in our imaginations with the greatest historic performers in the world. We were all too aware of the honor and the import of our opportunity.

There is a giant, golden-amber-stained glass "drop of light" skylight in the center of the ceiling, serving as the sun of the theater. This skylight is surrounded by a heavenly chorus of stained glass figures depicting singers of the ages. In the middle of Palestrina's piece, I looked up at that fixture and was overcome by the sight and the enormity of the moment. I have been moved before in the streams of music and continued singing; but this time I welled up and choked for a few measures until I could settle. Later, our ACFEA guide told us she had never before known of a group being allowed to sing in the Palau. She had heard that the director was on vacation and the guide would probably have been fired if it became known he had allowed us to perform on stage.

Our concert tour had been leading up to the Barcelona Cathedral that evening and, with four concerts accomplished, and growing familiarity with one another, we felt ready for the big moment. However, we started rehearsal tentatively, with the orchestra arriving a half hour before our scheduled time. Jo Anne hastily took her place and greeted the musicians, and here we again observed the pressure and responsibility of a conductor leading a new orchestra in a new setting. The Cathedral was hot and the lighting was below par.

Kate would label the mood of the thirty musicians as "stroppy" and most of us observed them to be less than professional. The orchestra manager played the cello and, although he turned out to be a competent musician, had ideas of conducting the chorus himself; during the first part of the rehearsal he tapped his foot and grunted to a beat sometimes other than Jo Anne's. The piece depended on the organ, and that player was perched in a loft high above us all, and unable to see Jo Anne even on a television monitor. Fortunately, he was an experienced musician and, although mostly following along, performed admirably.

The chorus was grouped in tight spaces and some could see only part of Jo Anne. A dolly clarinetist sitting in front of us basses fidgeted and flounced, rolling her eyes and flirting with the French horns sitting behind her. The horn section lacked full attention and Jo Anne gained their respect by flatly refusing to allow them to leave early, even though they had no notes in the last movement. Choral conductors are aware of orchestra players' biases against them in favor of instrument conductors, and European musicians still tend to a bias against female conductors.

With all these sub plots, Jo Anne set to with a strong will and soon had the orchestra in reasonable concert mode, enabling her to tune the chorus to the Cathedral acoustics. She rose to the challenge in that rehearsal, earning the respect of the orchestra and our continued confidence, love, and admiration. She also set us up for a great concert.

Jo Anne once mentioned that, in very rare instances, she has felt the chorus leading in a tone or tempo that was not of her choosing. She then adapts to the chorus rather than forcing them back to her direction. This decision is made to produce the best piece of music without interruption, rather than impose a direction that might lead to confusion. Likewise, on a tour such as ours, with new singers and unfamiliar orchestras, she would make the decisions of what needed to be fixed by her leadership, and what could simply not be put right in the time and talents available. These are rapid and crucial decisions, and perhaps why we survived five concerts in Spain with ourselves and the audiences feeling we had made satisfying music, even if strict examiners from the Julliard School of Music might frown somewhat. However, in Barcelona, Jo Anne firmly took charge and kept a tight rein on orchestra, chorus, and, to the extent she was able, the distant organist.

I had found a spot to stand toward the edge of the basses in what turned out to be the best possible location. To see Jo Anne better, I had packed two thick books in my backpack for a personal riser. All my favorite strong singers, Bob Lally, Jeff Warlick, and the UC Alumni Music Director, Mark Sumner were beside and behind me. Happiness is performing with the best. And to my delight, daughter Hayley and granddaughters Fiona and Georgina were immediately to my right. For the first time on the tour I was able to hear all three clear and beautiful sopranos in my right ear, almost persuading me to be silent in my enjoyment. I was able to see Kate happily ensconced in the alto section from my perch on the books that also gave me a clear view of Jo Anne.

And here I need to write a confession. As a new singer, unsure of my abilities, I have sung in concerts with my head buried in my score, seeking safety and reassurance, and not following the leadership of the conductor as a competent choral singer should do. Closely reading the notes and rhythm on the music page was a refuge and bulwark against the haunting prospect of making a mistake. Gradually, as I experienced progress in singing, and increased confidence, my head has come up and taken notice of my fellow singers and conductor.

Such a confession as this could only jeopardize my next audition, but I really am getting better. On that night in the Barcelona Cathedral, singing the beautiful and familiar Faure Requiem, and standing on my books with a clear line to Jo Anne, I found myself following her closely and using my music score only as a prompter. I listened and blended my voice with the chorus as never before. I felt I was growing in my singing, and the feeling brought great satisfaction.

That evening we gathered in the back of the vast Cathedral, assembled in concert lineup, and then marched in single files up two narrow staircases in the back of the altar area. The various audience spaces were filled to capacity with many watching on television monitors from otherwise obscured corners of the ancient cathedral building, and the assembly applauded us as we took our places. The orchestra exuded a welcomed new purpose and professionalism, appearing to be ready and positive. Apparently both Jo Anne and the chorus had won their respect, and they were ready to play their best for and with us. That is not to say all problems went away. At one time, in the first movement, the orchestra was on one cadence, the organ on another, and the cellist on a third. It took a few measures and stern looks from Jo Anne to pull everyone together.

It seemed to me that the chorus could do no wrong that night, and we all sang out with confidence and joy. When a chorus is relaxed and confident they will focus on the conductor, and the sixty-eight of us were following Jo Anne closely. Her Society members have come to read her moods and her slightest gestures. She has only to look at the bass section and raise an eyebrow and we all in unison exclaim to ourselves, *What?* and adjust accordingly. Her expressions and her hands tell us what we need to know and we depend on her. That night in the Cathedral in Barcelona, she communicated the message that we would sing together and we would sing well, and we did. Coming in exactly on the correct milli-beat, and coming in precisely with one's neighbors, is a pleasure and phenomenon that does not always come my way; but it did that night, and, I believe, for nearly all the chorus. We were listening to one another and singing as one.

Sometime during the concert we realized that this would be our last time singing this music together, and we all made the most of the moment. To use culinary terms, our chorus music seemed delicious, and we savored the notes and our tone. We enjoyed a splendid ovation, felt the sadness of the tour ending and, after, repaired to a table in the vast Cathedral square where a cold beer had never tasted better. Spain had indeed been a memorable experience.

Chapter Twenty-One

GOOD COMPLINE

● ● ●

COMPLINE IS THE LAST scheduled office, or ceremonial observance, designed to conclude the daily cycle of prayer in the monastic order with a quiet, meditative service, and blessings for a safe night. Where Evensong would be held in the late afternoon or early evening, Compline would be at night, at the close of the day's activities. One priest described Evensong as the mirror image of the Morning Prayer, and Compline as the spiritual expression of, "Now I lay me down to sleep..." The service is usually part of monastic orders and seldom used in parish churches.

My nephew, formerly Benedict Boulton and now Brother Chad, is a Benedictine priest and monk in the Ampleforth Abbey in the north of England. His order is attached to a famous boys' school where Compline is the most popular service attended by the boarding students. This experience reflects the Episcopal

Christ Church in New Haven, near Yale University, where a stu-
dent-led choir leads a 9:00 p.m. service when the college is in session. Compline seems to appeal to students and younger people.

* * *

Compline has become a well-known feature of St. Mark's Cathedral in Seattle. Kate and I made a point of attending the service we had heard about, and were not disappointed. We arrived
at 8:00 p.m. to hear the rehearsal for the 9:30 service. Fifteen men
ran through the new pieces that would be included that evening,
sight-reading, and picking up the notes and melodies quickly, with
the conductor fine-tuning the emphasis and pace. We realized that
these were accomplished singers and were very good together. A
friendly and talkative usher welcomed us to seats at the rear of the
nave where the singers would stand. He told us we would be surprised by the congregation, and he was right.

Twenty minutes before the service, a congregation with an av-
erage age in the early thirties, began streaming into the cathedral.
The young people quietly entered, many taking their places on
blankets they had brought, and some draping themselves around
the high altar area like seals on a rock. A meditative silence was
kept as the pews and floor space filled with a few hundred attendees, a surprising turnout for that time of night. We felt that this
was a regular congregation who knew why they were there and, in
their focused stillness, very much looked forward to the service.

Eventually, the fifteen men silently filed in wearing dark choir
robes, and took their places behind portable lectern barriers,
wheeled out for the purpose in the rear of the nave. A technician
worked the radio equipment for their weekly local broadcast. No
priest or service officiant, other than the singers, was in evidence,
and the service began with a lead singer intoning the opening

phrase of the a cappella prayer. There were no announcements, instrumental accompaniment, sermon, collection, welcome, or service sheet. The service of prayers, confession, Psalms, anthem, and concluding blessing were all sung, mostly in Latin. It was a rare and moving occasion, and was followed with total attention and appreciation by the large audience.

At the conclusion, the singers filed out quietly and the congregation made their way silently into the night. Some of the young couples held hands, and some groups who must have been regulars went off together.

* * *

In AD 596, a young priest, later to become St. Augustine, was sent from Rome to convert a wild English province. Expecting to be martyred by fierce pagans, he instead enjoyed great success as a missionary and later became the first bishop of England, headquartered in Canterbury. A few centuries later, in 1170, another archbishop, St. Thomas Becket, was martyred in Canterbury Cathedral because he disputed with King Henry the Second. Throughout history, worship and drama have continued in that splendid Cathedral, which is currently the seat of the Anglican presiding bishop. Just as in Chaucer's famous *Canterbury Tales*, every modern Anglican and Episcopalian should try to make a pilgrimage to the famous shrine.

One Sunday while we were in London, Kate and I woke up early with a spur-of-the-moment inspiration to drive to Canterbury. We arrived early, in time for a cup of coffee, and walked through the ancient Cathedral to the somewhat awkwardly raised choir and high altar area. In my best California accent, I asked an usher, who looked like he might be the Archbishop himself, if we could sit with the choir. This was not an unusual request, as most cathedrals will allow a few visitors to sit in the choir stalls, if space is available. We were fortunate enough to find seats next to two alto lay clerks, or professional singers, in the choir of sixteen men and twenty boys.

The service was all that we could hope for in the senior Anglican cathedral. The dean presided, and the theme of the day was a harvest thanksgiving with abundant decorations of farm produce. The processional hymn was, "We plough the fields and scatter the good seed on the ground..." Everything, even the sermon, was accomplished very well, but our outstanding memory is of the music. The setting of the mass was by a contemporary French composer, Jean Langlais, with an anthem by John Rutter. We were carried away into music euphoria from that splendid choir resonating in the famous building.

We all have a critical facility, deep within our inner being, that is the ultimate arbiter of an event. The critic either wants the performance, lecture, or whatever, to be finished so we can get on with life, or wills the event to continue. We cannot overrule or beguile that inner critic despite our opinion of the importance of the occasion. More than a few times I have been ready for church services to be over before it was, in fact, over. On that morning in Canterbury I longed for the service to go on forever.

A year later, I had a very different, but equally interesting, experience in the Cathedral. On our way to Austria, we spent the night in Canterbury before driving through the channel tunnel. Kate stayed in the hotel while I braved the night to attend a Cathedral Compline service that was quiet, austere, and without any music except for two hymns sung by the small congregation. It was a great comedown from the former choir music to sing a congregational hymn in the historic arches and choir section. There was a hint of ancient spirits in the cold, dark shadows of the Cathedral spaces during the spoken service. After, I walked away from the massive towers through the dark, cobblestone streets toward the hotel feeling as if I needed to look over my shoulder.

* * *

Perhaps the finality and the somber nature of Compline makes Evensong a far more appropriate service for the retirement age while one is still active. Compline is too reminiscent of the burial service to be appealing to a retired, active couple. If I found the Canterbury service to be difficult for my advanced years to contemplate, I could be certain that a memorial service would be far more challenging. Many find that sentimental emotions are more debilitating as we age, and I, for one, who cannot speak at a friend's funeral service for fear of becoming emotional, wonder if I could ever sing at such an occasion.

When a close friend died in late 2011, our St. Mark's choir was scheduled to be part of his funeral. I knew I would not have the emotional stability to speak or read at the service, and I wondered if I would be able to sing. Years ago, I was on a canoe fishing trip in northern Alaska and heard a lonely wolf cry. The whining, crooning, reverberating howl penetrated the mists of the lake and green hills and valleys with a dominating, earth-sorrow presence. I missed my pal greatly, and I feared that my voice would be the wolf's. During the service, the lump in my chest remained, but did not rise to my throat, and I sang, even though the excellent music for once was not an enjoyable experience. The memorial service was reminiscent of Compline.

* * *

In Cambridge, Massachusetts, there is a jewel of an Episcopal Church: the monastery of the Society of St. John the Evangelist.

The Episcopal monks and priests in the church, living facilities, and guest quarters maintain a constant spiritual presence and daily routine of prayer, contemplation, retreats, and spiritual guidance. The monastery serves as a beacon and source of strength for many Episcopalians, and an inspiration for church music, with continually sung services. It is gratifying to know that the secular, intellectual bastions of nearby Harvard University and the busy streets of Boston are continually bombarded with prayers from the monastery, including the daily service of Compline.

Every night at 8:30, the ten or so monks who are in residence, and perhaps a dozen visitors from the public, will quietly congregate in the beautiful chapel. The Superior will begin the service with the prayer, and then leadership alternates among the brothers. The hymns, Psalms, and prayers are sung and chanted in a manner to encourage a slowing and calming effect for the night. After the service, a silence is kept in the monastery until 9:00 the next morning.

Perhaps there will come a time in Kate's and my life when the Compline service holds more appeal, which will, for us, signal an expression of less active retirement. Until then, Evensong is our service.

Chapter Twenty-Two

ENGLAND SINGS

●　●　●

KATE'S ENGLISH BROTHER, John, and I share the unspoken knowledge that has long been a concern for him, and that I have come to accept: I am unworthy of his sister. The fact that we have been happily married for fifty-three years is a mystery to him and a joy to me, but he wonders when she will discover my deficiencies. John is an experienced singer and he knows that, among these deficiencies, I would never have the talent to be accepted by a serious choral group. For this reason, he was amazed when I told him of our plans to undertake a long musical sojourn in England. Of course he was not around for the years of extensive lessons and three seasons with the Santa Barbara Choral Society that had prepared me, and Kate, for such a trip.

On a previous trip to England, we had visited the headquarters of the Royal Society of Church Music in Salisbury, and one of the directors, Catherine Clark, gave us an inspiration to make the extended musical trip. This organization, founded in 1927, has grown to be a major support group for English singing with workshops, awards, publications, and every conceivable inspiration to church and cathedral music. Their USA branch inspires America as well.

After a good amount of research, we devised a plan to spend three months in England, singing as much as possible. The first requirement was that I would audition and be accepted by a major English chorus. I dreaded the audition ordeal, but it turned out to be positive and I was accepted by the London Chorus, as described in the "Verdi Moments" chapter. One can hardly imagine what that successful audition meant to me. Singers are always needy of validation, but rarely receive even a fraction of the amount they need. I was suspicious that my place in the Santa Barbara Choral Society may have been helped by friends and our support of the arts. However, this was an English audition held by the London Chorus conductor, Ron Corp, with no idea who I was other than a wandering American applicant for the bass section. When I was accepted, every practice and lesson to shape my unworthy talents had been proven worthwhile, and my confidence received a substantial boost.

With the chorus venue secured—assuming that Kate could pass the audition, and she did—our next problem was where to live in England. With incredible luck we found a couple who were friends of friends and also up for travel adventure. We exchanged their apartment in Barnes, a London suburb, for our home in the Santa Ynez Valley for the three months, and we were on our way. Once in England, we began our singing in earnest. After establishing ourselves with the London Chorus, we became extraordinarily fortunate to be recruited by the Bart's Choir, as described in the "Verdi Moments" chapter, then asked to join a combined chorus to sing *Carmina Burana*, and additionally accepted to join in with the Guildford Cathedral Singers. We had our hands full and we loved it!

The country sings everywhere. Young and old, sacred and secular, good voices and medium good voices, are heard throughout the land. The highest order of chivalry existing in England is the Most Noble Order of the Garter. Once a year they meet at Windsor Castle for a service of thanksgiving, and Kate and I were honored to be invited by our old friend and Knight of the Garter, John Sainsbury. On the big day, we dressed appropriately, including Kate's gorgeous hat, assembled our credentials, invitation, and directions, and arrived on time to be seated in the Chapel of Windsor Castle with an assemblage of important invitees. The Queen, the Duke of Edinburgh, Prince William, and most of the Royal Family would be in attendance for this traditional event which has continued in some form since 1348.

The Chapel is known for its boys' and men's choir and the service was graced with splendid choral music as well as congregational singing. We all sang the national anthem, "God Save the Queen," and two hymns, "City of God, how broad and far..." and "Be thou my vision, O Lord of my heart..." and the choir sang a Te Deum by Edgar Day, and an anthem by Herbert Andrews. The Windsor Chapel Choir was, as expected, very accomplished, but more gratifying was the volume and quality of the congregation's voices. Kate and I are accustomed to our own volume when in a congregation, but this time we found ourselves members of an enthusiastic common choir. It was exciting to be singing in a congregation that was able and willing to join in strongly. This was the highest order of chivalry, and they all had voices.

In April 2011, Prince William and his beautiful Kate were married in Westminster Abbey with all English pomp and circumstance. The marriage ceremony was a true service, complete with two anthems sung by the choir and also the highly coveted guest list singing "God Save the Queen," "Jerusalem," and two hymns, "Guide Me, O Thou Great Redeemer," and "Love Divine, All Loves Excelling." The Abbey Choir, supplemented by the choirboys from Windsor Castle Chapel, was expected to be very good, and they were, but additionally, the congregation led by the Queen sang with enthusiasm and musicality. God surely loves all the parishes dotted around England, large and small, but He must have experienced an additional pleasure to hear the top of English society belting away with gusto!

* * *

On our visit, Kate (not Prince William's Kate) and I took a road trip across the English countryside to see the sights and listen. We drove from London to Cambridge University to start at the top, with King's College Chapel, founded in 1446 by Henry the Sixth. The chapel is one of the architectural gems of the world. Additionally, the King established and endowed the King's College Choir to sing daily services, including Evensong, and they have been singing ever since. The choir is made up of sixteen boys, who have scholarships to the local King's College School, and fourteen men—four countertenors, four tenors, and six basses, all of whom receive scholarships to attend Cambridge University. The competition is keen, and the auditions and commitment serious, but the benefits for education and background to the boys in school and men in college are well worth the daily burden of rehearsals and chapel singing. Evensong is at 5:30 p.m. and a very good reason to make the trip north from London. Kate and I met a pleasant Cambridge Don, John Adamson, who escorted us past the line waiting outside King's Chapel for the Evensong service, and placed us in the choir stalls. The famous choir singing Evensong was a step on the way to Heaven.

* * *

Our next destination driving across the country was Oxford, where we paid our respects to the famous street where Cranmer, Ridley, and Latimer were martyred. Driving the English country-side on this beautiful day was a delight and, with only one or two wrong turns, we reached the impressive Norman-built Gloucester Cathedral. Among the lengthy and dramatic history of this Cathedral is an interesting fact. A son of an eighteenth century organist, John Stafford Smith (1750-1836), was a choirboy who went on to write a musical piece called "Anacreon," which became popular in America and ultimately the musical setting for "The Star Spangled Banner." Is it possible to imagine an English Cathedral choirboy who composed something that initiates every baseball game in America? As mentioned in the "Verdi Moments" chapter, we arrived much earlier than the 4:30 Evensong and ran into a dress rehearsal of the Verdi *Requiem* which we surreptitiously enjoyed, pretending to be part of the Cathedral staff.

That night we stayed at a country hotel in Cirencester and the next morning attended morning service at a large country parish where they tried to asphyxiate Kate with an over-generous incense censer. Again we noted the lusty volume found in most English churches where the two of us could sing to our hearts' content without standing out, as we would in some American Episcopal churches with a more modest hymn output.

* * *

On another very English visit, I was able to join the choir of the Parish Church of St. John the Baptist in a small town in the

London suburbs called Pinner. The church was modest by definition. The visitor's leaflet reads, "The village of Pinner was never
of any great importance and no wealthy or influential medieval
family ever resided in the parish." And later, "It is a very simple village church which has been described as one more of the all round
typical minor Middlesex churches."

I had called the choir director ahead of time and introduced
myself as wanting to attend the Evensong, a regular Sunday evening service. When I arrived early, he insisted that I sing with the
choir, which I did with some trepidation. The choir was five men,
four women, and seven young girls and boys. We had a short rehearsal in the choir room, after which we all donned choir robes,
and processed into the church with a congregation slightly smaller
than the choir. The service was beautiful in the old church, with
the choir singing well and me scrambling to keep up with the responses, Psalms, anthem, and hymns. I found the service precious
and meaningful, and will always remember the quiet Evensong
presence in that small church.

* * *

A road trip to the West Country took us to the historic town
of Bath. Romans settled in the town sixty years after the birth of
Jesus, with a community that became a center of pagan worship.
Some three-hundred years later, the town was a Christian center,
but the power and leadership struggles between Christians, pagans, various kings, Anglo Saxons, and Normans continued for
over a thousand years. Finally, Bath Abbey emerged to be a center
of the Anglican Church and the landmark building thrived until
the German Air Force bombs did serious damage in 1942. Today
Bath Abbey stands strong and splendid, a flourishing church and
also as a center for music.

Our nephew, Jonathon Boulton, an eye surgeon, and his wife, Nicky, hosted us to an ambitious Abbey concert. The City of Bath Bach Choir, with the Bath Camerata Group and the Wells Cathedral School Brass Ensemble, performed Monteverdi hymns and Psalms and the Chilcott *Salisbury Vespers* to a sellout crowd. Interestingly, the Camerata was ranged in the rear of the large abbey and the choir and brass were arrayed in the chancel at the front. The two performing groups would alternate, singing by themselves and then blend their voices across the length of the nave. The Camerata seemed to have the quality edge. The Abbey staff believes that music is integral to worship, and, in addition to numerous visiting concert performers and music education programs, maintains an ambitious choir with boys and girls choristers recruited from local schools to sing with an accomplished men's choir. We all felt uplifted by the concert and sailed out of the ancient church to stroll the fascinating and historical central town.

* * *

The English tradition of singing and participation allows the country to do many musical events. Members of church choirs rejoice when seeing that an anthem by John Rutter is planned because his compositions are always interesting, melodic, and will bring compliments from the congregation after the service. Rutter is a Cambridge man, a singer, a musician, and best of all, a prolific composer. *The Evening Standard* said, "For the infectiousness of his melodic invention and consummate craftsmanship, Rutter has few peers." Fortunately while we were in London, "A Day With John Rutter" was advertised as an organ fund-raiser by the Temple Church, and I paid my twenty-five pounds contribution to attend.

Alexander the Great was a natural leader who could muster and inspire his troops to accomplish great deeds and conquer the world. Of similar talent but more gentle charisma, John Rutter is also a natural leader and, on the Temple Church occasion, was able to conduct and inspire some hundred-and-fifty disparate singers into producing music far better than our untutored abilities, and do this in very rapid order.

That morning, we all crowded into the church, paid our twenty-five pounds, and settled into our sections, wondering who our neighbors might be, and could they sing? We immediately plunged into a section from Rachmaninov's *Vespers*, and Rutter cast a spell over all of us to sing as a chorus and perform well in no time at all. I particularly enjoyed his instructions to the tenors and basses. In one section where we had a double forte dramatic line, he told us to give it everything we had; he would tell us if it was too much. He never told us. The day filled with music from his own compositions, and that evening we sang a "concert" to ourselves that was credible. This type of spontaneous singing is a regular event all over England, and the Temple Church had another adventure to offer on our trip.

* * *

When Kate and I arrived in England for our three-month sojourn, we engaged a singing coach, Andrew Sackett, to improve our skills and keep up with the volume of music we hoped to perform. We were fortunate to have found him because not only was he a pleasant personality and extremely helpful, but he also invited us to join in a unique concert. Two musicians had established a partnership called "City Music Services" to organize choral clubs in large London corporations. Five of these companies, law firms Allen & Overy, Blackrock, and Freshfields joined with consultants KPMG and Rouse & Co. to pool all their amateur singing talents and present a concert of *Carmina Burana* in the historic

Temple Church, again to benefit the church organ restoration fund. Among his many other teaching and conducting situations, Andrew Sackett led the Freshfields law firm chorus and was scheduled to conduct the combined choruses in *Carmina Burana*. When he learned that Kate and I had sung the piece, he urged us to join in.

In 1803, a treasure of medieval poems, songs, and dramatic texts was discovered in an ancient Benedictine Monastery. Gradually, the words of these items were translated from Medieval Latin and old German into modern German. Twentieth-century musician-composer, Karl Orff, set some of these works in a dramatic musical piece titled *Carmina Burana*, described in the "Community Voices" chapter. The work was radical for its time, but has since become a favorite of choruses and audiences worldwide. In 1185, the Temple Church was consecrated in London as the British home for the Knights Templar. These knights were warrior monks who fought to protect pilgrims traveling to and from the Holy Land after the First Crusade. In 2010, Kate and I were to experience the incredible thrill of performing the medieval-based music in a medieval church.

We had only weeks to relearn the piece and would have only one rehearsal with the combined chorus. We set out with Andrew's help. The music is dramatic, rhythmic, and tricky to sing, but having mastered the piece once, the relearning came quickly. There is a men's section, "In Taverna," that goes four-hundred miles an hour, and if I studied over it once, I studied over a few thousand times. I ate and dreamt the words. Kate had some equally dramatic soprano sections; she and, I am sure, our apartment neighbors still hum the music.

At rehearsal, it was obvious that we had some very good voices among the lawyers and accountants who had also found time to learn the music. There had been some joint rehearsals in the various firms that we missed, and each time the companies had tried to outdo one another in refreshments and libations. Company pride was at stake, and Kate and I had fun figuring out who was who as the lawyers and accountants each tried to claim us. Everyone was very friendly and up for the concert.

The Temple Church is famous as the spooky set for the film, *Da Vinci Code*, with tombs of knights recumbent on the floor that bore their prone sculptures. We were placed to sing standing among the long-gone Knights Templar with the audience seated in the nave. The accompanying instrumental musicians were a specialty group called the "Carmina Ensemble" consisting of two pianos and a number of percussionists. Professional singers performed the solos and a group of children from Stepney Greencoat School filled in with angelic tones that only the young can produce.

When performing time came we filed into a packed church filled, no doubt, with members of all the firms wondering what their colleagues were up to, but all contributing to the organ fund. The opening notes are bold and loud, and we set off with a will, right on beat and pitch. I knew from the moment we began that we had a winner. The pianists attacked their instruments with inspired fury and the percussionists beat the hell out of their various drums and devices. The soloists caught the mood and outdid themselves, and the children chimed in with ethereal delight. I had visions of the dusty knights below vibrating and enjoying the musical reprise. There was a broad smile on Conductor Andrew's face, the audience loved us, and the organ fund prospered.

After, in the Great Dining Hall of the Inner Temple law courts, surrounded by the portraits of England's former Lord Chief Justices, we joined our daughter Hayley and grandson Ben, visiting from California. Hayley knew her insane parents were having the time of their lives singing this wild piece of music, and Ben had been impressed to be on the *Da Vinci Code* set with all the supine knights. The lawyers and accountants and business types enjoyed a glass of wine and mingled, very pleased with themselves. I knew that Monday morning there would be many feet still tapping under desks.

* * *

Our fall trip continued to be a feast of English tradition. Sunday, November 14, 2010, was marked as Remembrance Sunday in England, similar to our Memorial Day, to observe and honor all British military who have perished serving their country. Kate and I spent the day with two memorable experiences, first in a great cathedral and then in a parish church.

St. Paul's Cathedral held a formal Service of Remembrance as only the English know how to do it. The impressive building, first used as a place of worship in AD 604, was full of well-turned-out civilians and military, many with private and personal remembrances, and all with a dedicated, patriotic demeanor. Kate and I took our places with well over a thousand in attendance. The British have a sense of ceremony and serious intention on these occasions that is famous the world over, and indicative of a strong character and national pride. The venerable St. Paul's was the perfect place for the ceremony. The famous building had suffered greatly during the German blitz. Who will ever forget the dramatic pictures of the great Cathedral dome, bombed and burning after a Luftwaffe raid?

The processional hymn, "All people that on earth do dwell, sing to the Lord with cheerful voice..." was sung while flag bearers, the choir, the clergy, the City of London Aldermen, the Lord Mayor, and His Royal Highness Prince Michael of Kent processed to their places. The service included honoring all branches of the military and a commemoration of the fallen that clearly had a special meaning for many in the congregation. Those in the military sat together in groups and some held photographs of fallen comrades from their units to be remembered in that service. After watching the character and purpose of the ceremony and attendees, one could understand why England has never been conquered.

Shortly after the first ceremonial service, there was some shuffling in the vast Cathedral, and the second service, a memorial Eucharist, was celebrated, accompanied by the choir singing the Maurice Durufle *Requiem*, interspersed with the liturgy. The mood of the congregation was perfectly reflected in the formal Mass and poignantly spiritual requiem. Kate and I are fortunate, having lost only a few friends and no immediate family in war, but the service clearly brought home the sadness of those who have experienced tragic losses from conflicts. As the inspirational service continued, we felt as one with those in the Cathedral who were grieving for family, close friends, or fellow unit members.

After, as we stood on the steps of St. Paul's, our spirits were lifted by a Coldstream Guards parade setting off down the street. They were complete with tall bearskin hats and gray overcoats, stepping out on the cold November day.

That evening, we attended a very different, but equally British, remembrance. Kate's brother John, the one who had been a chorister at Winchester Cathedral—who could really sing and knew I could not—had discovered a poster advertising a "Flash" concert. All Saints' church in Putney is a large suburban parish outside London. To benefit the "Help for Heroes" British Veteran's Assistance Foundation they had conceived a "come one come all" performance of Gabriel Faure's *Requiem*. There would be a small orchestra and conductor, and anyone could sing in the chorus for a twenty-pound contribution. Brother John decided to go along with the performance as he had sung the piece many times and challenged me to learn it in ten days. It was an offer I could not refuse.

Kate and I scrambled to find the music score and a recording, and began working with our coach, Andrew, to prepare to meet the challenge. The Faure Requiem is a medium-length, uncomplicated piece, but still a struggle for someone of my experience to learn quickly without weeks of repetition and coaching. We discovered later, while singing the piece with the Choral Society on our trip to Spain, that this requiem is full of subtleties and nuances that require close attention and rehearsals to perform well, but we were only concerned to get through the Putney concert alive. We spent a hard few days listening to the recording, picking out the notes on the piano, singing through the sections for the benefit of our apartment neighbors, and working with Andrew.

Later that Remembrance Sunday, in the evening after our impressive St. Paul's experience, we proceeded to All Saints Putney where we met with a friendly church committee who gladly received our contribution and ushered us to the bass and soprano sections in the nave. Fortunately, John sang tenor, so he was removed from my friendly section and not available for critical review. At length, about one-hundred-and-fifty singers assembled, facing the small orchestra and conductor on the chancel steps. There was some hubbub as friends greeted one another and joined new neighbors in the sanctuary.

The conductor waved us into silence and, after a welcome from the event chair, said, "Let's turn to the second movement, pick up at measure sixty-four, and see what we have got." What she got was an amazingly coherent and competent sound from the assembled company that was not that far from a trained chorus. She stopped us after a couple of pages and admonished, "Not bad, but do try to watch me and stay on my beat." She then ran us through other sections with a few comments and repeats and, after some brief work with soloists, said, "I think that will do fine. Let's take a break and assemble back for the concert in twenty minutes." The break was enthusiastically anticipated and involved many cases of wine that were sold by the glass for a two-pound contribution. The Remembrance Day Fund prospered.

In the brief rehearsal, it was obvious that some first-class professional singers had shown up as well as some competent amateurs. The casual type singers sang softly, and the competent amateurs, such as I, filled in to round out the chorus. The attitude was casual but the outcome was a very creditable sound.

During the break, Kate, John, and I congregated at the busy wine table and I congratulated him, "Well, it is a pleasure to sing with a dedicated, well-rehearsed, and sober chorus, but at least I know now what a flash concert is!" Better yet, as we stood around making conversation and consuming wine, a substantial audience crowded in, paid their contribution, bought their glass, and took seats outside the chorus area in every available space in the large church. On reassembling, I noticed at least one glass of wine on the prayer book shelf in front of each bass, awaiting a break from our part so we could toast the sopranos or altos getting on with their parts.

When we all settled, the event chair again welcomed the audience and thanked everyone for the successful fundraiser and remembrance observance. The conductor raised her baton and we launched into a serious and well-performed requiem. Kate and I both agreed later that, even though we had managed only limited preparation of the music, and were singing with strangers, we both enjoyed the experience immensely and thought we had carried our parts reasonably well. Attempting a serious singing part, without extensive and precise rehearsal and coaching, was new ground for me. The audience gave the singers an enthusiastic ovation but, of course, we realized that the attendees were mostly friends, family, and congregation. With two very different events, Remembrance Sunday was well observed.

Our fall sojourn confirmed that choral singing is alive and well all over England, on many levels of expertise and support, and we treasure our memories, both participating and listening. Our high points were singing Verdi with the London Chorus and Bart's Chorus, *Carmina* with the pickup singers, and Evensong in the Guildford Cathedral. We returned home with a musical glow, and more confidence in our own singing abilities. We rejoiced that we could have such an amazing adventure at our time of life.

Chapter Twenty-Three

Delayed Honeymoon

● ● ●

In midsummer, 2011, Kate and I felt like a honeymoon couple planning our getaway trip. Once again, we signed up with the Berkshire Festival that had taken us to Montreal. This time we would travel, in September, to Austria and perform Haydn's *Creation Mass* in the Salzburg Cathedral.

Salzburg! Founded by the Celts in the fifth century, capital of the Austro-Hungarian Empire, home of centuries of great music and festivals, and recently home of the von Trapp family of *The Sound of Music* fame. Mozart played in the ancient cathedral founded by St. Rupert and St. Virgil and now the one-hundred-and-fifty singers of the Berkshire Festival would sing their Sunday Mass.

The Berkshire organization sent us the sheet music and a learning CD in order for us to prepare the piece prior to arrival; so

Kate and I, along with reading our guidebooks, began studying our Haydn. We are all familiar, from our school days, with the student who was given high praise for effort, but a considerably lower grade for execution. That might well describe my music career, with an "A" for effort and a "Hope to pass" for performance. I have learned to live with that and began to study every day for the Salzburg concert. My favorite practice spot in our home is a corner with a table, comfortable chair, good window view, and handy CD player. I turned on the music and went over it time and again until I practically knew it from memory. Additionally, I would sing at least twice a week with the ever-patient, and infinitely helpful, choir director, Rose Knoles. Gradually, as in the case of the Montreal Berkshire week, I learned the Mass and other motets we were to sing separately. The process was not a burden and I actually enjoyed the slow practice and improvement. Kate, in her head-of-the class fashion picked up the music and chirped away her soprano line with considerably less difficulty.

Finally, we flew to London and a couple of days later made the long drive to Austria and our headquarters hotel, fifteen miles from Salzburg, where we arrived two days before the Festival schedule for some sightseeing and acclimatization. The hotel was built from a monastery in the small town of Mondsee on a picture perfect lake in the Austrian Alps, immediately adjacent to the town square with welcoming outdoor cafes where waitresses wear gorgeous dirndls. It is dominated by the ancient St. Michael Basilica where we would sing the motets on Saturday night before the Sunday Mass in Salzburg.

The Basilica was the setting for the wedding scene in *The Sound of Music*. On the same chancel steps where Julie Andrews married Christopher Plummer in the film we would sing to the town just after the Saturday evening Mass. The famous Basilica was founded, well before the film industry began to define our culture, in AD

748, on a location that probably experienced a variety of pagan worship going back well before recorded history. According to the Basilica guidebook, the golden age of St. Michael's began around 1400 and lasted until the attached monastery was dissolved in 1791. The cathedral-size church has survived wars, revolutions, confiscations, occupations, and secular onslaughts. Through all this history, daily services have been held in greater or lesser form in the church, and now would be filled with one-hundred-and-fifty earnest American voices. We do not realize always that we are living history, but we are.

The chorus gathered for the first rehearsal in a large, acoustically lively convention hall, with the performance eight days away. The friendly bass section took seats in their designated chairs and shook hands, pleasantly chattering and wondering who we all were, and could we all sing? Vacationing lawyers, bankers, Air Force Colonels, professors, and miscellaneous retired folk sat down together with one purpose. Kate and the sopranos chattered away with enthusiasm, as sopranos do, until we were all brought to order.

The Berkshire Festival president, Debbie Kennedy, gave us welcome words and introduced our director, Thomas Bottcher, who would be our pilot, and who soon captivated the attention and affection of the assembled chorus. His resume includes many choral, symphony, and teaching posts that belie his youthful looks and enthusiasm. He had conducted over five-hundred performances of the Vienna Boys Choir. He was obviously an impressive man, but his assignment now involved pushing a trainload of disparate voices, who were otherwise on a singing holiday, up the tonal hill to arrive in just over a week with choral brilliance to a critical Salzburg audience at their weekly Mass. Mozart and Haydn had performed here and they took their music seriously. We began.

The Festival staff, ably led by music director Frank Nemhauser, strongly believes in a thorough voice warm up, and each day a section leader guided us through stretches and exercises before any voice sounded. We reached for the ceiling, twisted our necks, massaged our chins, rotated our shoulders, and finally shaped a note. The scales and vocal exercises took us above and below our normal singing range and comfort levels with a shape and accuracy that prepared us to sing better than we ever had.

Teachers and conductors search their imaginations to inspire their chorus. We were exhorted to spread our arms, as though to hug our neighbors, and then fill the space with the sound of the hug. We must color our voices with pastel hues and paint the ceiling. We must project through the tops of our heads, and place the tone before our eyes, heading for the front wall. We were to be swans paddling on a serene pond, our lower diaphragms serving as the paddling energy beneath the surface, and our voices the gliding creature above water; all must be peace and forward motion with aesthetic perfection. Peculiar images, perhaps, but as the days progressed, the magic seemed to work and the tone improved.

A couple of days into rehearsal, however, left most of us frustrated and concerned when the great sounds were elusive and the pace Thomas required was faster than any of us believed attainable. The Latin came to us easily, but the German of the motets was a problem for some of the chorus. He was herding cats, and the notes and rhythms seemed to sidle out of unity and cohesion even though Thomas pushed us with every ounce of his being. He led us onward with a manly, energetic demand to the bass section; a flirting, tiptoe coax to the sopranos; a pleading wooing of the altos; and a theatric gesture and exhortation for the tenors. The musical markers moved slowly toward a performance. He never singled out individuals, but an occasional grimace sent an admonition of pace or tone to a deficient neighborhood who felt the guilt and strived to please. Our brilliant accompanist occasionally emphasized a note or chord that hinted a sure sign that we had gone astray.

Gradually, but surely, we melded into a chorus tone, and the look on Thomas's face when we grooved with his leadership was worth the effort. For an hour most mornings we were divided into voice parts for section rehearsals, and the bass section worked with Frank Nemhauser, a first-class singer himself and a gifted teacher. The men grew daily in their ability to produce a Mass in Salzburg and also in their confidence with themselves. We will never know what Thomas Bottcher and the section leaders truly thought about their singers' quality, but we believed that, surely, they must think we were improving. On the sixth or seventh day we began to sound like a chorus.

Our first performance was to be a set of motets in the Mond-see St. Michael's Basilica. We began to look forward to the performance with a confidence and pleasure we had not felt a few days previously. We took our places on the chancel steps for dress rehearsal and, as usual, I was with the taller types at the top of the steps in the far back row. This position was far removed from our conductor and, as some of us silverbacks suffered from hearing loss as well as attention deficit, we missed some of Thomas's direction. Additionally, he stood in semi darkness in a black shirt, so we took much of our direction from his facial expressions. We asked for a white shirt for the performance, which he duly wore, except he also wore his black coat. Fortunately, we were well rehearsed and could anticipate his moves, and also had the beautiful motets well in mind.

We all have succumbed to involuntary emotions that manifest themselves in physical reactions, whether sad or pleasurable, but out of our control: a father watching his daughter in her marriage ceremony; the funeral of a close friend; certain passages of music that evoke emotion, all produce physical reactions that are very real and stimulate avoidance or attraction. Sometimes we experience a tingle—chills; sometimes a welling of tears; sometimes, on the negative side, an intestinal revulsion, but always a very real reaction.

Recent scientific study has made progress in quantifying the musical circumstances that inspire listening pleasure. A musical device, called "appoggiatura," involves combinations of volume, timbre, and harmonic pattern that create a conflict, then a resolution that satisfies the listener and induces the release of dopamine, a chemical that gratifies the brain. If the pattern is set up correctly, and is combined with an inspirational text, the result will be a good feeling, possibly manifesting chills and tears. Why certain individuals are more susceptible than others to the emotions of music, and why different compositions appeal to different people, is still the subject of endless discussion. But the fact that music inspires emotions is well established.

A particular motet on our program, "Heilig Geist," or "Holy Spirit," a contemporary piece by Augustus Kropfeiter, moved me greatly. We sang: *"Atme in mir, du Heiliger Geist, das ich Heiliges denke,"* or "Breathe in me, O Holy Spirit, that my thoughts may all be holy." The music and words brought great pleasure to me every time we sang the piece; even writing about the experience moves me emotionally. Others in the chorus responded to other sections of our program, but "Heilig Geist" caused chills down my back when we sang it.

Beyond that, being a part of a chorus in full volume—whether the *Carmina Burana*, Verdi's *Requiem*, Brahm's *Requiem*, or "*B Minor Mass*"— double forte moments of full chorus, bring indescribable, soaring pleasure to me.

Similarly, in certain compositions, the double piano, softly sung passages, when the chorus gets it just right, have brought more gently felt, but equally impactful, pleasure and emotion.

Choral singing is a feast of delights that keeps on giving.

All of us in that Mondsee basilica Saturday night felt a pleasurable anticipation to be singing and looked forward to the Salzburg Cathedral the next morning. We formed up in the large vestry room, then walked onto the steps in prearranged order, starting with the tallest. The top-of-the steps basses had moments to stand and observe the crowd as everyone else filed onto the steps below. We could see that the Basilica was full of people who closely watched these Americans who had been sitting around their street cafes in Mondsee, drinking coffee and beer, and consuming strudel and pretzels. Our program of motets and contemporary modern German songs progressed straight through without applause, but with a standing ovation on conclusion. We sang well without any mistakes and were pleased with ourselves as we milled into the cast party at the adjoining hotel, with a pride of accomplishment. However, the celebration was somewhat muted because we anticipated the challenge of the Haydn Mass in the Cathedral the next day.

* * *

Prior to our evening concert, we all had bussed into Salzburg for a dress rehearsal with the orchestra that was waiting for us as we crowded into the Cathedral. We took some time to find places on the bank of risers that had been provided in one of the transepts, but there was an overflow, and twenty or so altos stood on the floor. The orchestra was seated on chairs, with music stands, in front of a side aisle, and Thomas conducted from the edge of the pews. We were ushered by cathedral functionaries and observed with curiosity by the crowd of tourists who continually streamed through during our rehearsal.

The ascending, white-walled interior featured four organ lofts, one on each massive corner pillar that led up to the great dome, where Mozart had played for the congregation. The four soloists took their places in one loft, high above the chorus and orchestra in a somewhat precarious perch. There was, for once, good room for all of us and we settled in to sing while gazing at our incredible surroundings.

High hanging chandeliers were suspended in space by interminable chains. Art, decoration, and architectural features piled on top of one another reaching for the vaulted ceiling. The vast building presented a feast of saints, angels, apostles, cherubs, benefactors, skulls, gospelers, historic clergy, doves, candles and candle holders, pietas, chapels, crucifixes, pillars, balconies, moldings, glass, pulpits, confessionals, bishop's stalls, clergy stalls, choir stalls, paintings, sculptures, and more, joined by soaring architecture, gilt metalwork, and marble. The Cathedral was a festival of Baroque masterworks and we meekly stood to make our offering to the history, sanctity, and treasures of the legendary edifice. Thomas brought us down to earth with a businesslike rehearsal, mostly concentrating on the soloists and orchestra, all watched and photographed by wandering Cathedral visitors. Thomas told us that he was pleased and reminded us to drink water and get a good night's sleep.

On Sunday morning Kate and I rose early, packed, and checked out because we planned to drive to Vienna immediately after the concert and needed to park the car somewhere in Salzburg during the Mass. Everyone else rode the bus to the Cathedral with plans to train or plane their separate ways. We fretted about losing our way and where to store the car, but all went smoothly and we found ourselves with leisure time.

A coffee shop on the cathedral square provided the best coffee and pastry of my life, and we wondered if Mozart had similarly paused before a concert. We two old birds perched and reveled in the sunlight and gazed at the copper-green-topped great dome and twin towers. Pre-performance jitters had long ceased to be a part of our lives, but we did feel an anticipation and excitement as people, who were to be our audience, filtered through the square and wandered into the Cathedral. The great doors were flanked by four massive statues of St. Peter and St. Paul, and the Cathedral founders, St. Rupert and St. Virgil. A procession of horse-drawn tourist carriages arrived to set up shop, and other early risers joined us in our street café, lured in by the bakery smells.

Eventually the crowd picked up and a congregation seemed to be wandering in for early seats. Finally, the chorus arrived like a flock of meandering birds, dressed in black pants and skirts and white shirts and blouses, clutching black music holders. Show time.

We gathered in the generous transept space behind the risers, and noted the orchestra sounds as they tuned up behind the heavy doors of a side chapel. The Berkshire music director, Frank, lined us up and we took our places as the thousand-plus congregation filled the pews, with some standing against the opposite wall. The soloists sat on chairs in their high balcony and the orchestra settled into their seats. A Mass sung by a one-hundred-and-fifty-member chorus and concert orchestra, led by a famous local conductor, was not unusual for the musical city of Salzburg, but we could feel an excitement of anticipation and, perhaps, a curiosity about what these Americans would do for their town and church.

The congregation rose when the elaborate and colorful ecclesiastical procession entered from a side aisle behind the altar. Two incense bearers led, followed by crosses, acolytes, servers, and, finally, a number of priests quietly making their way around and then through the congregation to the vast altar area. After the presiding priest intoned the opening words, Thomas rose on cue, raised his arms, and gave us a conductor's look. During the procession I glanced around at the thirty or so fellow basses, focused and determined, and the bright-eyed Kate poised and prepared for flight. We were ready.

The Mass began with the violins, three beats per measure, right on, with chills going up my back. I took a couple of deep breaths from my lower diaphragm, then envisioned the sound shaping in my body and sailing out of the top of my head. Next, four measures of alto solo initiated a countdown as fraught and decisive as a space launch. One measure to go and my mind flashed something St. Paul wrote to the Ephesians: "Sing and make music in your heart to the Lord!" Our note was a natural F, easy, beautiful, forte, on the beat; share it, the words "Kyrie Eleison..." or "Lord have mercy..." done. We were away. What joy!

Our voices and orchestra filled the historic spaces as had been done in some form since AD 673, when the missionaries arrived, through 1728 when the foundation stone for the Cathedral was laid, and as will be done into the future. To be a visiting American chorus contributing to this succession filled us with a great satisfaction, and we performed well.

We followed the format of the Mass, singing the Kyrie and Gloria, pausing for the words of the Mass, then the Credo, another pause, then the Sanctus, Benedictus, and Agnus Dei. We put our hearts into the music and performed well above any rehearsal. There was no reaction from the congregation because we were an integrated part of the Mass. During the announcements in German at the end of the Mass we sensed that the chorus was being introduced and we were acknowledged with brief, polite applause.

The sermon, delivered in German, was lost on almost all of us but brought us a welcome break. We were then allowed to sit in place, somewhat uncomfortably—I was leaning backwards, legs tangled in metal struts. With one leg asleep and unable to move, and the other threatening cramps, I had a long think about how to extricate myself while the sermon intoned. When the time came I devised a two-hands sideways pull, followed by a kneel, and then a major heave. Many of my less nimble and similarly distressed compatriots were given helping hands to bring them back into formation. Our elderly bass section must have resembled a biblical scene, but the lame stood to sing again.

During the performance, I had an experience that indicated I had progressed in my abilities, and which resembled a similar moment driving race cars. Years before I had driven an open cockpit and very lively Formula Ford on the competition circuits. Speed is measured in those cars by very slight details; in lap times, tenths of a second can make a big difference. If one comes out of a corner with a hundred extra revolutions per minute, the results will show in faster speed down the straightaway. At a certain advanced point in my brief racing history, I was able to be relaxed about skidding tires, walls rushing by, dancing competition pressing in the rear-view mirror, and other survival details, so I could concentrate on the RPMs. An upgrade from 3,700 to 3,800 in the safe negotiating zone on a certain corner could win a race, and the ability to notice the RPM dial amidst all the other rushing confusion indicated a mastery of the moment.

In a similar presence of mind that day, in Salzburg, I accomplished all the details of singing and was able to focus also on the musical presentation as a whole. I willed myself (and everyone else) to increase in quality of sound and derive just that little extra that would give us a great performance. In that Cathedral I had somehow achieved the presence of mind to go beyond the basics and into the total phenomena and participate with music, urging my tone to the best quality. It is a little farfetched to have a mental flash of race car competition, but singing brings out those moments.

After, as Kate and I said goodbye to Thomas Bottcher, he sincerely conveyed his pleasure with the performance. We told him we now understood why the acoustics, as well as Haydn's joyous enthusiasm for the Mass, required a fast tempo and careful articulation, and he complimented our chorus on both. Kate was accosted by several American tourists who had wandered in by chance and stumbled upon fellow countrymen singing in the city of music. They were very proud and moved by our presence representing our country and thrilled to hear us.

My father was appointed Ambassador to Belgium in the seventies and, visiting him, I became familiar with the diplomatic process. Conferences, receptions, formal visits, the busy work of a large staff, the occasional flaps, the security and Marine detachment, and other formalities are all the stuff of diplomacy, and doubtless necessary to maintaining friendly terms with other countries. However, it is difficult to imagine a better representation for our country than a choral concert. In Montreal, Spain, Italy, Germany, and England we had seen how well the audiences interacted with the singing Americans. In each case, the host-country audiences were always very friendly and appreciative of our being there and singing for them.

Kate and I enjoyed this brief honeymoon trip after our marriage fifty-three years previously. The excitement and joys of that newly married moment in our lives will never be repeated. However, for this retired couple, the Austrian singing trip will run a close second, and if less intense and exciting, was all the more enjoyable in our retirement years.

Chapter Twenty-Four

Sing On

● ● ●

THE LAST SUNDAY on our tour brought a return to Guildford. When the final hymn note from the morning service echoed in Guildford Cathedral, the silence brought Kate and me a sweet moment of satisfaction and happiness. This was the end of our 2011 trip to Austria and England, and our last scheduled opportunity to sing in the Cathedral. At our stage of life, one cannot depend on repeat performances, and nostalgia flavors moments of accomplishment and joy now with a realization that this is what it is, and not necessarily what it will be.

At the verger's signal, after the blessing, our choir bowed together to the altar then moved from our two choir stall sides, met our opposite in the center of the chancel, and filed out in twos, women first, followed by men. I watched the blue-robed Kate process before taking my turn. Our double file turned left at the bottom of the chancel steps before the silently standing congregation, then left again down the high arched aisle behind the altar area, and, after a pause for our dismissal prayer, down the stairs to store our robes and music sheets.

It is inconceivable to me that people shall not always remain in some state of motion. Hawaiian folklore envisions a myriad of night marchers tramping the islands through eternity. The stately, endless column is led by kings and high priests in flowered golden robes and high-crested crowns, attended by bearers of flaming torches. Ancient chants and stamping feet keep rhythm as the numberless procession winds through the dark. This image strikes a reasonable chord with my philosophical outlook, because I am sure in some way we shall always continue in motion, although it is not ours to know the details.

Our choir in Guildford had just sung the Cathedral communion service at 9:45 a.m. as well as the 11:00 Morning Prayer service, no small undertaking for an amateur group of singers. The other thirty or so choir members were familiar with the routine of the Anglican liturgy and had sung some of the pieces before, but Kate and I needed to refresh ourselves on the services and learn the music. We did at least feel part of the team and were recognized and welcomed because we had sung with them the previous year.

We secured the music two weeks in advance and practiced hard. A very talented tenor and choirmaster in the local Barnes church, Dan Turner, had agreed to take us both for lessons and was invaluable in preparing us with the music and details of the liturgy. The communion service included a sung Psalm, many pages of musical setting by John Ireland, and the anthem, "Holy Is the True Light" by William Harris. The Morning Prayer service was another sung Psalm, the "Jubilate" by Charles Stanford, responses by William Smith, and an anthem, "Give Us the Wings of Faith" by Ernest Bullock. The choir carried it all off without a hitch, and Kate and I drove back to London tired and pleased. We were ready for the next day's flight for California after two months away from home.

On arriving, we looked forward to a year with a very welcome absence of schedule, unlike the press of engagements and obligations that were routine in the earlier times of our lives. As with most retired people, we essentially had a blank schedule with little or no essential or obligatory fixtures on our future calendar. Our lives when raising a young family, and during my tire career days, had been closely scheduled around school-year requirements and business appointments. Later, the growing-up family and winery enterprise absorbed every minute of every day in the year. Political office, of course, presented a fixed and full legislative calendar. Now, in our senior moments of life, everything is discretionary, with very little demanded or required. The activities of thirteen grandchildren, the social and community events, and the never-ending options of charity fundraisers or good works, are all possibilities, but almost everything is optional. This retirement life can be both a blessed relief or somewhat empty, depending on the circumstances of the individuals involved. A retired life full of interesting pursuits can be a pleasure, and possibly the best period of our years; without activities it can be a downright debilitating, creeping disease of inactivity and boredom. Kate's and my situation reflects the universal conditions of retirement years and the need to provide real avocation and pursuits.

Our story in this book relates our extraordinary good fortune in stumbling onto choral singing. We found a retirement activity that is demanding, fulfilling, and infinitely fascinating for us and probably will add a few years to our lives in the package. Obviously, not everyone desires to take the time and effort for choral singing, or may not have the gift of voice. The point of telling our story here is to suggest that there may be an equivalent engrossing post-career avocation that has the potential for extra health and enjoyment for each one of us in retirement. Pursuing that dimension, either before, but certainly after, retirement is very much to be desired.

We must all be aware that there is a very real potential for a less than fulfilling partner relationship in later retirement years. With aging we will inevitably experience debilitating aches and pains, wakefulness, indigestion, blurred vision, and the concerns of diminished physical ability and activity. We are not as beautiful, able, or patient as we were in our more vital years, and these imperfections might grate on a relationship. The most obvious and universal frustration is hearing loss, and the inevitable irritation of repeating a phrase to a seemingly stubborn partner at the dinner table. Familiarity with a spouse's imperfections is a source of angst in the otherwise golden years. How much these debilitations and fading faculties bother older marrieds, or provide a subtle virus for a deteriorating relationship, depends on both understanding and activities.

For young newlyweds, the delights of a honeymoon trip serve to reinforce the sometimes tenuous relationship of the young, disguising any tremors in the new intimacy and commitment with the delights of travel and adventure. Likewise, in later life, the delights of mutual activity are able to help suppress or obscure the inevitable traumas of aging, which might intrude into the happiness of a couple. Everyone will do well to have their own Evensong time "honeymoons"; and for us it is choral singing. The ups and downs of rehearsals, the musical peccadilloes of our vocal neighbors, and the stress of performances all provide infinite interest and a source of private gossip and pillow talk. The honeymoon trip can be replicated with a passionate pursuit that might have infinite definitions for all couples, but singing did it for us.

Kate and I still love each other deeply and forever; however, there is no question that the very real business of living together has been enhanced and enriched by song. Our moments of learning music together, either sitting down at our table in front of the window with the CD player, side by side at the piano, or simply listening to each other singing away at a new composition, have brought us a shared purpose and delight. Mastering a complicated piece of music, to the best of our abilities, has brought us the great satisfactions of shared accomplishment. Best of all, after the preparation, excitement, tensions, and then the completion of a demanding and physically challenging performance, our relaxed exhaustion and pleasure is a mutual glow and reassurance that the best years are not behind us, but are now and in the future.

Our future singing schedule includes a Choral Society performance of Durufle's Requiem and Mozart's Coronation Mass with the Santa Barbara Symphony. On the more creative side, we are presenting a concert in a Santa Ynez Valley warehouse and a "flash concert" in a Santa Barbara Department Store. On the travel side, we look forward, next summer, to an Edinburgh trip for a Mozart Grand Mass with the Berkshire Festival. This is enough music to require extensive preparation and practice, which, fortunately, we look forward to and is an enjoyable element that fills a part of every day. We drive to choral rehearsal every Wednesday evening and rise early Sunday morning for choir rehearsal with pleasure. The Evensong period of our lives is, in fact, a song.

The outside world is not an optimistic place in these otherwise pleasant years, and perhaps in these retirement days we have too much time to contemplate gloomy newspapers and TV broadcasts. The economy of almost every country is in some degree of crisis, and a real possibility of financial collapse looms as a threat, without resolution or even definition. Political turmoil is a fact of life in many places, particularly the Arab world. In America, polarization threatens to override reasonable policy conversations, and thoughtful and objective political statesmen seem to exist only in the history books. There is talk of world-ending meteorites and population-decimating plagues. Every day brings some new indication of our culture and civilization sliding toward barbarism, if one were to believe the newscasters. The daily news is all the more reason to sing.

Similarly, in Geoffrey Chaucer's Medieval England, threatening tensions from sickness, war, social upheaval, and a myriad of dangers loomed and threatened everyone's life and dreams. From this background he wrote the compelling and enduringly popular *Canterbury Tales*, a bestseller and source of stories and illustrations for centuries. The image of a disparate group of people traveling on a pilgrimage together and telling stories to one another is a universal depiction of life. We all travel through our days, each in our way seeking grace from our pilgrimage, and each having stories to tell. Kate and I continue our life travels and, in this book, I have told our story. The path of mankind on innumerable separate pilgrimages will continue into future centuries, together with and despite the many threats to existence.

People who attend church often wring their hands and despair because of declining popularity of religion, the threats of legal and atheistic challenges, and cultural indifference leading to reduced membership and worship. Of course that attitude denies the reality of God, who is, and always will be, in our lives and world. Pagan competition, theological disputes, brutal religious conflicts, and indifference have always plagued, but never defeated the practice of religion.

Evensong continues as the spiritual and aesthetically delightful service in the late day. The substance, the words, and the music must and will continue to be available to the faithful. My own prayer and desire at my Evensong time of life has evolved from hoping for a future doorway sweeper position in the house of the Lord to a place somewhere in the back of the heavenly choir. And

I have every expectation something like that will, in fact, occur, ideally together with Kate in the soprano section and me with the basses.

The Evensong Service

The following pages record a standard rendition of the basic Evensong service that might be performed in any Episcopal or Anglican Church today. This service is the modern version of the Prayer Book written by Thomas Cranmer and introduced into the Church of England around 1549. With minor changes it was adopted in Elizabethan times and has remained as the evening service with few alterations. Cranmer replaced the seven offices, or services of the monastic order, with two daily services for churches, Morning Prayer and Evening Prayer. His purpose was brevity, clarity, and an important increase in the amount of Holy Scripture to be read in English.

The beauty and simplicity of the two services have been a source of satisfaction and success for the Anglican/Episcopal church over the centuries. The strength of the liturgy is that it remains constant and not subject to the individual creativity, emotions, or opinions of the local minister or evangelist. Herein resides one of the fundamental differences between the Episcopal Church and many other protestant denominations. Episcopalians prefer consistency, repetition, and a minimum of spontaneity or innovation in their liturgy. When I hear and participate in the Evensong service, I am doing that which Queen Elizabeth the First did, as well as my martyred ancestor, and so on down the generations to the present. When I attend St. Paul's Cathedral in London or St. Thomas's in New York City, I will pretty much find the same service.

Of course there are infinite variations of musical settings, and also freely chosen anthems, Scripture readings, and sermons. It can be a simple or elaborate ceremony, with either one presiding voice or many participants, lay people and ordained, performing the speaking parts of the services. What Episcopalians do not have is the sometimes questionable notions of individual pastors, other church leaders, or solo evangelists creating their own liturgy.

Anyone visiting London should place an Evensong visit high on their schedule. One cannot get a better sense of English culture, language, music, and spiritual soul than in St. Paul's, Westminster Abbey, or many other cathedrals and churches around the country. No Anglican/Episcopal credential or experience is required to attend. A strong recommendation is to check the schedules for the services in these magnificent institutions, for this is a must see. Similarly, the National Cathedral in Washington, and many Episcopal churches around us, are homes for splendid Evensongs.

Here is a travel tip for tourists abroad: when attending an Evensong service in a major English Cathedral, arrive for the service early and ask one of the formidable, but really very friendly ushers if a seat in the choir is available. The choir stalls have housed the royalty of the realm and important figures of the church for centuries, and sitting in one is to sit in history and also to feel an intimate part of the service. The ghosts have been praying at Evensong for centuries, and are quite harmless. One also might be placed next to the choir singers, something like being on the opera stage, but do not try to join in. I often wonder why so many tourists just visit sightseers' London when they can attend a cathedral service and live London.

The Evensong service, as written in the Book of Common Prayer, allows a number of variations, but what follows is a basic service. Sometimes the choir will sing an opening piece, which might be from the back of the Cathedral, before processing to their places. The Episcopal Daily Evening Prayer, or Evensong, opens with one of a number of suggested phrases. My favorite is from an Old Testament Psalm: "Worship the Lord in the beauty of holiness; let all the earth keep silence before him."

The priest then asks the congregation to confess by saying: "Let us humbly confess our sins unto Almighty God."

The congregation then says: "Almighty and most merciful Father; we have erred and strayed from thy ways like lost sheep. We have followed too much the devices and desires of our own hearts. We have offended against thy holy laws. We have left undone those things which we ought to have done; and we have done those things which we ought not to have done; and there is no health in us. But thou, Oh Lord, have mercy upon us, miserable offenders. Spare thou those, O God, who confess their faults. Restore thou those who are penitent; according to the promises declared unto mankind in Christ Jesus our Lord. And grant, O merciful Father, for his sake; that we may hereafter live a godly, righteous and sober life, to the glory of thy holy name. Amen."

The priest then declares absolution for the congregation: "The Almighty and merciful Lord grant you absolution and remission of all your sins, true repentance amendment of life, and the grace and consolation of his Holy Spirit."

All then say "amen," and say together the Lord's Prayer: "Our Father, who art in heaven, hallowed be thy name. Thy Kingdom come. Thy will be done on earth as it is in heaven. Give us this day our daily bread. And forgive us our trespasses, as we forgive those who trespass against us. And lead us not into temptation. But deliver us from evil. For thine is the kingdom and the power and the glory for ever and ever. Amen."

Now the choir, or congregation if there is no choir, or sometimes choir and congregation together sing the responses to the sung words of the presiding leader:

Leader: "O Lord open thou our lips."

Response: "And our mouths shall sing forth thy praise."

Leader: "Glory be to the Father and to the Son, and to the Holy Ghost."

Response: "As it was in the beginning, is now and ever shall be, world without end, Amen."

Leader: "Praise be the Lord."

Response: "The Lord's name be praised."

The appointed portion of the psalms which is to be used on that day is then read or sung. Typically when sung, the verses will alter from one side of the choir to another. Cathedrals will divide the choir into Cantorus, the left or Precentor's side when facing the altar (which is where Kate and I sat in Guildford Cathedral), and Decaus, the right or dean's side of the chancel. Here, for example, is the 23rd Psalm:

"The Lord is my shepherd; therefore can I lack nothing.

He shall feed me in a green pasture; and lead me forth beside the waters of comfort.

He shall convert my soul; and bring me forth in the paths of righteousness for his Name's sake.

Yea, though I walk through the valley of the shadow of death, I will fear no evil; for thou art with me, thy rod and thy staff they comfort me.

Thou shalt prepare a table before me in the presence of them that trouble me; thou hast anointed my head with oil, and my cup shall be full.

Surely thy loving kindness and mercy shall follow me all the days of my life; and I will dwell in the house of the Lord forever."

Next, a portion of the Old Testament will be read.

Then will be said or sung the "Magnificat," or the words from

St. Luke's Gospel that Mary spoke when she learned that she would bear a child who was to be called Jesus. "My soul doth magnify the Lord, and my spirit hath rejoiced in God my savior. For he hath regarded the lowliness of his handmaiden. For behold from henceforth all generations shall call me blessed. For he that is mighty hath magnified me, and holy is his name. and his mercy is on them that fear him throughout all generations. He hath showed strength with his arm. He hath scattered the proud in the imagination of their hearts. He hath put down the mighty from their seat and hath exalted the humble and meek. He hath filled the hungry with good things and the rich he hath sent empty away. He remembering his mercy hath holpen his servant Israel, as he promised to our forefathers, Abraham and his seed forever."

Then a portion of the New Testament will be read.

After that reading, the "Nunc Dimitis" is said or sung. These are the words, again from St. Luke's Gospel, that were said by a man called Simon who believed he would not die until he had seen the Messiah. He spoke these words after he had held Jesus, then a baby: "Lord now lettest thou thy servant depart in peace, according to thy word. For my eyes have seen thy salvation, which thou has prepared before the face of all people; to be a light to lighten the Gentiles and to be the glory of thy people Israel."

The congregation then states their words of faith: "I believe in God the Father Almighty, Maker of heaven and earth; and in his son Jesus Christ his only Son our Lord; who was conceived of the Holy Ghost, born of the Virgin Mary; suffered under Pontius Pilate, was crucified, dead and buried; he descended into hell; the third day he rose again from the dead; He ascended into heaven, and sitteth on the right hand of God the Father Almighty; from thence he shall come to judge the quick and the dead. I believe in the Holy Ghost; the holy catholic church, the communion of saints, the forgiveness of sins, the resurrection of the body, and the life everlasting. Amen."

Once again, the leader and the congregation or choir singing repeat the responses:

Leader: "The Lord be with you."

Response: "And with thy Spirit.'

Leader: "Let us pray. "O Lord show thy mercy upon us."

Response: "And grant us thy salvation."

Leader: "O Lord, save the State."

Response: "And mercifully hear us when we call upon thee."

Leader: "Endue thy ministers with righteousness."

Response: "And make thy chosen people joyful."

Leader: "O Lord, save thy people."

Response: "And bless thine inheritance."

Leader: "Give peace in our time, O Lord."

Response: "For it is only thou, Lord, only, that makest us dwell in safety."

Leader: "O God, make clean our hearts within us."

Response: "And take not thy Holy Spirit from us."

Next comes prayers, as appropriate. My favorite is: "Lighten our darkness, we beseech thee, O Lord, and by thy great mercy defend us from all perils and dangers of this night, for the love of thy only Son, our savior, Jesus Christ. Amen."

Then follows an anthem, chosen by the music director to fit the occasion. Next it is possible to insert a sermon, followed by the prayers and the blessing: "The grace of our Lord Jesus Christ, and the love of God, and the fellowship of the Holy Ghost be with us all evermore. Amen."

There is room in the design of this basic service to add variations, but only within the context of the service as written. Often, more modern language is used, but this is the structure of the Evensong service. It has served for hundreds of years, and hopefully will do so for many hundreds more.

Appendix Two
The St. Thomas Church
Evensong Description

The following description of their Choral Evensong is taken directly from the New York City St. Thomas Church description of Evensong:

"If you are not accustomed to our service, which is only one among many possible ways of worship, these notes may be useful. Our aim here is to offer beauty in stone and song to God, the giver of all beauty and goodness. Based on the services held daily in the medieval church, Evensong as arranged in the Book of Common Prayer of the Anglican Church has been sung regularly in our church since the sixteenth century, the Tudor age in England, with only a few breaks (during the commonwealth of the seventeenth century). Here the music is sung by the choir. You are asked to join silently in the service while they sing the prayers and other music which they have practiced with care. But we all join the choir in singing the Creed; in adding Amen to the other said prayers; and in singing hymns. Because we maintain this tradition of Evensong, you will find that we use in this service the old forms of the prayers and scriptural readings.

"After the introduction to the service, the choir recites the appointed psalms. We can think about the psalms, the hymn book of the Temple at Jerusalem, as our Lord Jesus Christ did when he used them; the words will be found in the middle of the Prayer Book. The lesson from the Old Testament follows. It is read from the Lectern in the English of the Authorized Version (1611). The choir then sings the Magnificat, the song of the Blessed Virgin Mary when the promise of the Old Testament came true (Luke 1). The lesson from the New Testament proclaims the good news of

Jesus Christ, and is followed by Nunc dimittis, the song of Simon when he had seen our Lord in the temple at Jerusalem (Luke 1). The service leaflet will show you which musician composed this setting of Magnificat and Nunc dimittis.

"All then stand, facing the altar used at the Holy Eucharist, and other reminders of the life of our Lord Jesus Christ. We sing together the Apostles Creed, the expression of faith of those who, generation by generation in the Christian church, respond to the gospel of Jesus Christ, crucified and alive."

Prayers are then sung by the priest and the choir. They end with the "Collects" which collect our thoughts. A hymn, sermon, and anthem may follow. The anthem is usually a meditation on a text of the Bible or in the old prayer books. The words of the anthem (including a translation if the words are in Latin) will be found in the service leaflet.

The End